Working and Writing for Change

Working and Writing for Change

Series Editors: Steve Parks and Jessica Pauszek
Associate Editor: Justin Lewis

The Working and Writing for Change series began during the 100th anniversary celebrations of NCTE. It was designed to recognize the collective work of teachers of English, Writing, Composition, and Rhetoric to work within and across diverse identities to ensure the field recognize and respect language, educational, political, and social rights of all students, teachers, and community members. While initially solely focused on the work of NCTE/CCCC Special Interest Groups and Caucuses, the series now includes texts written by individuals in partnership with other communities struggling for social recognition and justice.

Recent Books in the Series

UVA Untold: Black Women's Narratives at the University of Virginia, edited by Cheyenne Butler

Communities in Action: Creating Spaces of Social Change, edited by Yndalecio Isaac Hinojosa, Isabel Baca, and Jasmine Villa

The People Demand Democracy: Voices from the Myanmar Spring Revolution, ed. Pratha Purushottam, et al.

A Parent's POWER by Sylvia P. Simms

The Forever Colony by Victor Villanueva

Visibly (and Invisibly) Muslin on Grounds: Classroom, Culture, and Community at the University of Virginia, ed. by Wafa Salah and Fawzia Tahsin

The Lived Experience of Democracy: Criticizing Injustice, Building Community, ed. by Kaitlyn Baker, et al.

Steal the Street: The Intersection of Homelessness and Gentrification by Mark Mussman

Literacy and Pedagogy in an Age of Misinformation and Disinformation ed. by Tara Lockhart, Brenda Glascott, Chris Warnick, Juli Parrish, & Justin Lewis

Faces of Courage: Ten Years of Building Sanctuary by Harvey Finkle

Equality and Justice: An Engaged Generation, a Troubled World by Michael Chehade, Alex Granner, Ahmed Abdelhakim Hachelaf, Madhu Napa, Samantha Owens, & Steve Parks

Other People's English: Code-Meshing, Code-Switching, and African American Literacy by Vershawn Ashanti Young, Rusty Barrett, Y'Shanda Young-Rivera, & Kim Brian Lovejoy

Becoming International: Musings on Studying Abroad in America, ed.by Sadie Shorr-Parks

Dreams and Nightmares: I Fled Alone to the United States When I Was Fourteen by Liliana Velásquez. ed. and trans. by Mark Lyon

The Weight of My Armor: Creative Nonfiction and Poetry by the Syracuse Veterans' Writing Group, ed. by Ivy Kleinbart, Peter McShane, & Eileen Schell

PHD to PhD: How Education Saved My Life by Elaine Richardson

UVA Untold:

Black Women's Narratives
at the University of Virginia

Edited by

Cheyenne Butler

Parlor Press
Anderson, South Carolina
www.parlorpress.com

Parlor Press LLC, Anderson, South Carolina, USA
Copyright © 2025 by New City Community Press.

Library of Congress Cataloging-in-Publication Data on File

1 2 3 4 5

978-1-64317-527-0 (paperback)
978-1-64317-528-7 (pdf)

Working and Writing for Change
A Parlor Press series.
Editors: Steve Parks and Jessica Pauszek

Book design by Justin Lewis // justinlewis.me
Cover illustration by Autumn Jefferson

Parlor Press, LLC is an independent publisher of scholarly and trade titles in print and multimedia formats. This book is available in paper and eBook formats from Parlor Press on the World Wide Web at https://parlorpress.com or through on-line and brick-and-mortar bookstores. For submission information or to find out about Parlor Press publications, write to Parlor Press, 3015 Brackenberry Drive, Anderson, South Carolina, 29621, or email editor@parlorpress.com.

Contents

Common UVA Terminology

Institution
PWI - Primarily White Institution
HBCU – Historically Black College and University
Grounds – Preferred term traditionally used by UVA students, faculty, and alumni to refer to the university space in place of "campus".
Beta Bridge – Bridge on Rugby Road displaying student painted messages

Student Organizations
ALSO – Afro-Latino Student Organization
BSA – Black Student Alliance
EESA – Ethiopian & Eritrean Student Alliance
EJC – Environmental Justice Collective
ITCOMS – In the Company of My Sisters
MU – Muslims United
MSA – Muslim Student Association
MRSC – Mixed Race Student Coalition
OAS – Organization of African Students
PMP – Peer Mentoring Program for Latinx Students
SJP – Students for Justice in Palestine

Student Affairs Offices & Services
CAPS – Counseling & Psychological Services
HRL – Housing and Residence Life
OAAA – The Office of African American Affairs

Student Centers, Communal Spaces, Events
The Lawn – Community gathering area and green space in front of the Rotunda
Lighting of the Lawn – Students, Faculty members, and the UVA community gather with food and performance in December on the Lawn to celebrate the Rotunda lighting.
LSC – Latinx Student Center
MSC – Multicultural Student Center

Greek Life
AKA – Alpha Kappa Alpha Sorority Inc., historically Black Sorority (NPHC)
AXO – Alpha Chi Omega Sorority (ISC)
KKG/ "Kappa" – Kappa Kappa Gamma Sorority (ISC)

IFC – Interfraternity Council
ISC – Intersorority Council
"The Divine 9"/ NPHC - National Pan-Hellenic Council

Student Roles
RA – Resident Assistant
OL – Orientation Leader
PA – Peer Advisor (Black Students)

Majors, Departments, Programs, & Scholarships
Batten – Frank Batten School of Leadership and Public Policy
DMP – Distinguished Majors Program
GPH – Global Public Health
WGS – Women's & Gender Studies
Posse – Posse Full Tuition Leadership Scholarship Program
Ridley – The Ridley Scholarship Program

Acknowledgments

First and foremost, all thanks and Glory be to God.

Secondly, I would like to thank the wonderful and talented women of Black UVA who chose to participate in this project, telling their stories of becoming and belonging at UVA, a primarily White institution. They trusted me with their stories, and it was the utmost honor to edit and showcase their narratives to the world. I am forever grateful for them and the UVA Black organizations like BSA (Black Student Alliance) and ITCOMS (In the Company of My Sisters) for promoting the study. Without those organizations alongside UVA's Women's Center, I would not have had the participants that made this project possible.

This project would not have been completed without the financial support from UVA's Harrison Undergraduate Research Award. Therefore, I'd also like to express my gratitude to UVA's Undergraduate Office of Research. The office's Undergraduate Student Opportunities in Academic Research (USOAR) program provided me with the opportunity to work as a research assistant under the mentorship of Professor Stephen Parks, starting my second year. Without the USOAR program, I would not have had the initial funding for my research that made this project and my journey as an undergraduate researcher possible. Therefore, I'd like to thank Office of Undergraduate Research director Andrus Ashoo and former assistant director Melissa Hey for their endless support and insight as I navigated my undergraduate research journey and growth as a young professional.

I am forever grateful and blessed to have had former research assistant and UVA Alumna Angela Grey Theriot assist me with the project's initially daunting transcript editing and participant interview process. Her kind words, spirit, and expertise made collaborative aspects of this project as frictionless as possible and enjoyable.

I'd also like to acknowledge and give thanks to my research mentor, Professor Stephen Parks. From the very beginning he believed in the purpose and vision of this project and research from its inception and served as the ultimate mentor and guiding hand throughout all steps of the research, editorial, and writing process. He also provided me with all the wisdom, agency, support, and resources to make this book possible. All while ensuring I received the proper funding and compensation for my work towards the project. Thank you, Professor Parks, for believing in me and the importance of these Young Black Women's narratives and the necessity of their stories being told in their own words.

Thank you to the Posse Foundation for making my time at The University of Virginia possible. Posse has not only provided me with a prestigious education and an immense network of resources, but a cohort of peers who are now my family. To all my lovely friends (named and unnamed, you know who you are) thank you for your never-ending warmth and support. I appreciate all of the affirmations and kind words you've given me over the years in support of my research journey. I owe Sophia Hartshorn, Dawn Ford, Darnisha Augustin, and Mary Robinson the world and more for patiently listening to my research-related worries and woes as well as my triumphs and ideas. Iron Sharpens iron and I am immensely proud to have befriended four brilliantly intelligent, research involved young women during my undergraduate years.

Lastly, thank you to my beautiful family for your support, love, and occasional tough love. The women in my family, specifically my mother, aunt, and grandmother set the standard for me not just academically and professionally, but as a Black woman. Therefore, I am forever grateful for all that my family has poured into me and sacrificed for me to receive the education and opportunities they did not have the luxury of receiving themselves. They too deserve the world and more for listening to all of my woes and worries as I underwent my research journey with this project.

Introduction

Cheyenne Butler

As a young child in Lutheran pre-kindergarten, I remember a classmate pointed to the flesh of her light beige palm, proclaiming we weren't the same color. I looked at my palm. It was still beige but with darker palm lines due to my skin's melanin. I didn't get it; what was the big fuss? We weren't that different. However, apparently, to her and the other White and non-Black children who stood quietly nearby observing, my skin color was an issue.

I don't remember thinking much about that interaction as a young girl other than the other girl was weird and needed her eyes checked. Our palms were nearly the same color. Plus, we had played together before, and I'd always had the same color palms. Little did I know, it wasn't about the palms, and nothing was wrong with her eyes. I was Black. For the first time to my knowledge, some people apparently took issue with that fact. But it wasn't until some years later I realized I'd directly experienced racism early on as well.

I was nine the first time I ever spoke about it. I attended a local Black salon's retreat program for young Black girls. The program aimed to create a safe space for young Black girls to learn about skincare and haircare as well as to gain confidence. The day was filled with pampering sessions and vision boards. There was also a group conversation featuring a speaker about Black girlhood. The conversation veered into our first encounters with racism and mistreatment as young Black girls. One by one, we gradually began recounting times we'd been teased about our hair or told we were too dark. We recounted the times we felt unlikeable or explicitly othered. All of these events occurred at an early age.

The speakers' eyes widened as each girl told their story. She ended the conversation, stating that she was surprised by our experiences, noting that not as much has changed since she was a girl our age. However, this marked the first time I sat in a room of girls around my age who understood what I had been through, saw it for what it was, and ensured everyone's similar experience was heard. Our conversation did have moments of Black joy, which stemmed from pride in our community and identity as Black girls. However, it highlighted the persistent alienation many faced, especially in school or amongst our peers.

It wasn't until middle school that I attended a non-majority White institution. In middle school, two classmates and I went to a Barnes & Noble to work on a group project. Working on the task at hand, we kept our conversations quiet. A man who sat nearby observing us took it upon himself to compliment the mother who accompanied us about how we were "surprisingly well-behaved." He said these words with the sheer amazement of someone who has seen a dog walk on its hind legs. We exchanged wide-eyed looks with one another while the mother took the compliment with pride.

Perhaps the non-Black man really admired how we diligently worked together on Saturday afternoon. However, the fact that he went a step further and mentioned that he taught at a school that had a majority Black and Brown population made us immediately silently clock the "compliment" for what it likely was: racist. My friend's mother seemingly did not seem to see it that way. Often, many older generations of Black women took pride in a non-Black person's acknowledgment of how well they and their children subverted stereotypes and expectations of Black girlhood. The three of us were initially taught to view those interactions and backhanded compliments the same way. Yet that specific interaction planted seeds of doubt and questioning. Why must other Black girls be put down to compliment us? Why, as Black girls and women, are we responsible for subverting the stereotypes that others created for us? Why do we sometimes internalize the gaze and viewpoints of others? I carried those thoughts with me as I entered high school, my first institution with a substantial Black population. The school served as a formative, nurturing, and validating experience for me. I finally existed in an educational space where no one asked about my hair or how I spoke. I was one of many. The connections I made with my Black peers through friendship provided the start of my exploration of my relationship with Black femininity and girlhood.

I entered the University of Virginia (UVA) – a primarily White institution - during a pandemic and social justice movement. For the first time, I wondered more deeply what being a Black woman meant to me – beyond the challenges associated with being Black and a woman in America. What was my relationship to my community…the Black community? UVA marked the first time Black individuals from diverse ethnic and socioeconomic backgrounds surrounded me. I knew how my experiences and upbringing crafted my reality as a Black woman, but how did theirs? From the Twitter diaspora wars to proclamations of Black unity, what it means to be Black is a focal point of discussion within the community. Blackness means so much more than the absence of whiteness. Therefore, I began to intensely wonder: How do we, as Black individuals, let alone Black women, understand ourselves? How does the world see us? But more importantly, how do we see ourselves? What experiences have shaped that understanding, and how does all of that vary across socioeconomic classes and the African diaspora?

***

During my second year at UVA, I became a research assistant with the Undergraduate Student Opportunities in Academic Research (USOAR) program, which allowed me to research these pressing questions regarding UVA's community of undergraduate Black women. To begin, I had to know and understand the Black UVA women of years past. This research revealed the presence of Black students and women years before their formal admission to UVA, but what we knew about them and their experiences was finite. In *"It was about time: A timeline of women at UVA"* I found a detailed timeline of the presence of women at the institution.[1] Although it doesn't specifically focus on Black women, I came across the name, E. Louise Stokes Hunter, the first Black woman to earn a UVA degree in 1953. Then through a presentation by former Maxine Platzer Lynn Women's Center director Abby Palko, I discovered that a Black woman studied on grounds before Dr. Stokes-Hunter. Her name was Isabella Gibbons, a Black enslaved woman on UVA grounds who later became a Freedman and a Jefferson school educator, was the first woman to learn (as in acquiring knowledge by studying academic materials) on UVA grounds. Again the documentation was finite.

I became curious about the history of Black women at the institution, specifically their educational and social experiences. What were we missing? More importantly, what has been done presently to memorialize and document the experiences of Black women at UVA? To gauge the contemporary experiences of Black female students, I read a post on Orphee Noir, a Black student-run publication from the UVA Office of African American Affairs. There, I found the article *"The Cultural Divide of Partying,"* which gives insight into the still largely culturally segregated social spheres of Black and White students as well as how a Black undergraduate female chooses to navigate said spaces.[2] This was the only article I found that addressed the social experiences of Black women at the institution.

Historically and presently, I discovered there was a general absence of comprehensive research and testimonies of the Black female student experience at UVA. As an institution, there is a gap in our understanding of what it means to be a Black woman at UVA, how their identities have shaped their experiences on grounds, the communal spaces they've built, and contributed towards. There are no existant studies of how they narrativize their social/academic experiences and interactions with peers. This gap has allowed a normative conceptualization of the "college experience" that is profoundly enmeshed within, and a product of, an assumed White cultural atmosphere. As a result, many of the cultural and communal touchstones of university life, especially at UVA, are experienced and documented through the lens of White students. This White cultural atmosphere manifests itself through the prominence of things like White Greek life and secret societies. Clearly, UVA has a well-earned reputation as an outstanding institution. However, its total value can only be discussed by recognizing the contributions and experiences of marginalized and undervalued populations.

It was within this context that I undertook this book project, which documents the academic and social experiences of Black female undergraduate students at UVA. *UVA Untold* explores through personal testimonies how current undergraduate Black female students comprehend their experiences at the University of Virginia and how they seek and form a community on grounds. These testimonies also provide an avenue to examine how their experiences exist within the greater framework of the university historically erasing the contribution of Black women on grounds. *UVA Untold* explores the following key questions: How do undergraduate Black female students understand their experience at an institution like the University of Virginia? What experiences, past and present, have formed that understanding of their experiences at the institution? To discover answers to these questions, a participatory ethnographic methodology was used. Specifically, the primary means of gathering information was through a series of private one-on-one informal interviews with Black female undergraduate students at the University of Virginia main campus. I constructed specific questions for participant interviews.

- What does it mean to you to identify as a Black woman?
- Prior to attending UVA, what experiences have shaped your identity as a Black woman?
- Prior to attending UVA, how did you imagine the ways your racial identity would shape your UVA experience? What was your actual experience?

- Prior to attending UVA, how did you imagine your UVA classroom experiences? What was your actual experience?
- Prior to attending UVA, how did you imagine the ways in which diversity is defined on grounds? What was your actual experience?
- Prior to attending UVA, how did you imagine your potential community? What was your actual experience?
- Prior to attending UVA, how did you understand yourself as a Black woman? Has that understanding now changed?

For the purposes of this project, I've defined Black female undergraduate students as any women-identifying student of the African diaspora who self-identifies as Black and is currently enrolled at the University of Virginia as a first through fourth-year student. This definition includes Black female students with multi-ethnic and racial heritages, as long as participants self-identify as Black and are closely descended from the diaspora. Such a definition of "Black" affords community representation holistically as they interact and organize on grounds.

Participants were recruited anonymously, primarily through organization list-servs and word of mouth. Prior to the interview, participants signed an IRB consent form. The intentionally informal interviews mirrored casual conversations, so participants felt comfortable while discussing heavy subject matter. Other researchers might have used qualitative methods for this study. They might have taken the surveys, made charts, and analyzed data on an Excel sheet data. However, I did not want to make these fifteen women's experiences into data points. I wanted them to show everyone who they were. Yet also how they've experienced the world and UVA as Black women through their own words. Once interviews were recorded and transcribed, they were uploaded to a secure location. Transcribed interviews were coded by noting recurring themes and edited into narratives.

Seventeen interviews were initially conducted and transcribed into narratives. However, two individuals retracted their participation in the study. They noted they no longer felt comfortable publicly discussing their experiences and interactions with university peers and organizations. Their decision was tied to fears about possibly causing issues within the university community as well as a possible lack of anonymity, given the information expressed in the narratives regardless whether a pseudonym was used. Those two individuals understandably were concerned about backlash and decided against sharing their stories publicly. Other participants also expressed concerns surrounding privacy and anonymity due to the personal nature of the narratives, which in many participants' cases included open criticism against the institution, faculty, and peers. Therefore, four participants used pseudonyms to obscure their identities while omitting any easily identifiable aspects of their identities or relationships with organizations and individuals to further protect their privacy. Those requests highlight common concerns of marginalized people when openly speaking against an institution and racism. The fear of retaliation or harassment remains a genuine concern, as it has happened to individuals who have critiqued institutions like UVA. Therefore, I fully respect the participant's narrative retractions and the request for anonymity. All of which were respected and implemented accordingly.

The ordering of the narratives in this book is deliberate. The narratives are ordered in a manner that presents growing complexity in identities and institutional critics as the book progresses, while also providing an arch of thematic cohesion and narrative flow.

Those with similar identities often precede or succeed one another to indicate contrasting viewpoints and experiences while also enshrining commonalities. For example, the book starts off with Neveah and Alexis, two young African American women from Virginia and similar backgrounds. While later narratives from Kasey and Jackie, who share similar social circles due to being ISC members, have contrasting social experiences and takeaways regarding life as Black women at the university.

The narratives showcase a hyperawareness by these Black women surrounding how non-Black individuals perceive them in primarily White university spaces. Thus, these narratives present knowledge and a communally tacit understanding of their own "otherness" even when the perpetrators engaged in unintentional othering or dismissive behavior. Gabrielle shared, "When me and my friends are out in UVA just being Black and minding our business, it definitely does attract a lot of stares." She also noted that while studying or passively enjoying time with her Black peers on grounds, "People do have a tendency to either stare or completely ignore your existence, especially in study spaces." Such moments often entailed students "talking really loud, being a little bit disruptive." All of which demonstrates how she remained hyper aware of non-Black students' hyper-observation and disregard of Black students in university spaces.

Furthermore, Black women in this study often noted the invisibility of their presence in academic spaces. Alexis mentions "times where White students, who are the majority in the class, feel as though their voices are more important than yours." She further noted that in classroom discussions, "It's like they're not allowing me to speak." However, participants who expressed their lack of inclusion by peers in classroom conversations and group work often exercised their right to call the behavior out. Mackenzie, a first-year student, mentioned a situation in a chemistry study group where a White student suggested that she and another Black student were not "pulling their weight" equally. Mackenzie immediately replied by telling her, "You're not gonna need to carry me. I can do all this work on my own. And what you said wasn't very nice and respectful, so let's just work as a group, get this done, and we can move on."

Invisibility and ostracization for Black female students also occurred outside the classroom, typically in social spaces that White students often frequented. In T.N. 's narrative, she mentioned how, "There are certain frats that I know that Black women or just women of color in general, you're not going to go there if you're over 120 pounds. You're not going to this frat because they're not going to let you in." Neveah's narrative also addresses the possibility of objectification and mistreatment in White frat settings that only seemingly allow Black women entry. She mentions how in the "the two times that I've been to White frat parties, I've been objectified by White men" after they observed her dancing in a fashion that is typical at Black parties. The frat members incorrectly saw the dancing as an invitation to harassment and unwanted touching. Not all participants interacted with the university's party scene. However, those who primarily acknowledged the party scene's racialized differences expressed greater comfort in Black-hosted frat parties and social settings. Kendle, in her narrative, stated, "I'm usually more comfortable being who I am when I'm surrounded by other Black people cause when you're surrounded by White people, I sometimes might feel like, oh, I don't want them to perceive me differently or negatively just because I'm Black." Many Black women experience a level of comfort and freedom of expression in Black social spaces. That comfort was often only possible to varying degrees in White dominant spaces, as described by Neveah and Kendle.

Another component of social interactions discussed by Black women in this study was relationships on a college campus. When it comes to dating and romantic interactions with peers, the personal narratives describe dating at UVA as entirely different for Black women than White women? Arianny's narrative expresses how her dating experience at UVA "has just been a joke." She explains how many believe that "UVA is where you're meant to find the love of your life. I'm like, not if you're Black." T.N. also shares a similar sentiment and attributes her own and other Biracial and Black women's difficulty with dating at UVA to its primarily White institution (PWI) status. She states, "I think the beauty standard here for women in the nicest way possible is stick thin, White, blonde hair. I'm not that, so it's very hard to feel desirable by a big part of the UVA population." Collectively, then, the narratives suggest that many of the social spaces deemed standard and a part of the quintessential "UVA experience" are overwhelmingly White. All of which isn't an immediate "shocker" given the school's status as a PWI. Black female student's interactions with these textbook UVA spaces, should they choose to inhabit them, more often than not, are met with challenges and difficulties on account of their race and gender.

Hence, many students noted finding support for such efforts through the small yet tight-knit Black student community, organizations, and social spaces that provide a space of free existence and expression. Arianny stated in her narrative, "The amount of support and energy I've received from the Black community here at UVA is unmatched." Participants like Taylor specifically mentioned how her friendships and community with other Black women at UVA posed an incredibly validating experience that contributed significantly to her personal growth while at the institution. Participants stressed the presence of Black community unity, especially during challenging events at UVA that impacted the Black UVA community. Participants like Taylor and others discussed the statue of Homer Noose and the The Office of African American Affairs (OAAA) Vandalism Incident. On September 7th, 2022 a hate crime investigation with FBI involvement ensued after someone placed a noose around the Homer statue's neck. This incident was especially jarring given the noose's symbolic meaning of racialized violence against Black Americans through lynching, which was even acknowledged as such in President Jim Ryan's message to the university community hours after university security personnel discovered the noose.[3] That incident occurred just weeks after the University Police Department reported vandalism at OAAA after finding broken windows at Dawson's Row.[4] Anxiety and demands for transparency arose within the UVA community as the university shared limited information regarding the investigation of the two incidents.[5] Gabrielle marked those incidents and the ensuing protest as something that rallied the Black community and strengthened community coalitions with other minority student organizations. Therefore, the importance of organizations such as BSA and spaces like OAAA and The Multicultural Student Center (MSC), among many others, is highlighted throughout the narratives. These organizations and spaces serve as places of refuge with support systems through programming and events tailored to Black student's needs and interests. All of these demonstrate the value, success, and necessity of these university offices and initiatives for the well-being of marginalized students.

However, many, if not nearly all, participants remained staunchly critical of UVA's commitment to diversity and the services, as well as the resources offered to students, especially those hailing from marginalized communities. Many characterized UVA's commitment to diversity as performative or limited. In her narrative, Nicole mentions, "I don't think the university is committed to diversity in the sense it wants to be. I still do very much think that, in so many ways, diversity is just a checkbox that they can check and say, "Yeah, we have this person." Throughout the book, narratives echo that UVA does not have an expansive view of diversity, often thinking of it in terms of race as opposed to socioeconomic class, gender, and orientation. While few narratives acknowledged other forms of diversity, the majority commented on how much of the UVA student body comprised of those with financial privilege. Which is a largely correct assumption. As of 2023, less than 15 percent of UVA undergraduates hail from low-income families.[6] According to many participants who identified themselves as low-income to middle-class, wealthier students displayed their wealth through expensive clothing like *Golden Goose* coats and vacations throughout the year. Additionally, the experiences of one participant who hails from a more affluent background illustrate how wealth, its racial dimensions, and perceptions of socioeconomic class can be influenced by the community one inhabits.

Most participants also remained critical of the university's origins as an institution but argued for the importance of their presence on campus. Many of them were aware of the university's intertwined relationship with slavery and the oppression of Black and other marginalized communities, too. One participant, C.R., even mentioned that they were descended from the enslaved laborers at UVA. Therefore, many narratives express the common theme: Despite the institution's history, we are still here. In her narrative, Neveah expressed that, "Existing here in this space, taking up space as a Black woman at the University of Virginia, is itself a big FU to the institution of racism and the institution of slavery and Thomas Jefferson, all of this." Thus, she sees her presence and other Black student's presence at the university as a form of resistance.

Another common theme for participants was addressing the collective struggle that is especially faced by Black women when discussing what Blackness and Black womanhood meant to them. They view their experiences within a shared history of the Black women and individuals that came before them. - one that links them all past and present. Many view their role in the struggle as difference-makers within the Black community who uplift Black girls and women as others have done for them. A core component of their identity is resistance and resilience. They want all Black women to be seen as complex individuals and not limited to stereotypes and expectations. This remains especially evident when participants like A.D. mention how "Blackness is a lot more complicated than stereotypes and a lot more complicated than what may be the most common experience. Not identifying with common experiences does not make me not Black. I don't have a choice in that sense." As a result, the narratives represent an array of individuals with deep connections and understanding of themselves as Black women or their Blackness. However, the narratives also present the journeys of those who are still in the process of exploring their Blackness, especially as biracial women. This provides further intricate insight into Blackness, Black expression, and how it impacts the student experience at a primarily White institution such as UVA.

***

The goal of this book is not to define Blackness or womanhood. Nor is the book's goal to ascribe any set universal experiences to all Black undergraduate women at primarily

White institutions. While we are alike, we are all so different. Nor does the book aim to place judgment on those who are closer in proximity to Black culture and community than others. We all deserve community and the ability to inhabit spaces that respect us and cater to our individual needs. This book does not include reductive explanatory insight into the community. It is crafted to showcase the beautiful tapestry of women who make up Black UVA. These young women have a variety of personalities, experiences, and world outlooks. The narratives showcase their humanity and understanding of their complex identities. This offers further insight into diversity across the Black diaspora and aids in holistically understanding UVA student experiences and needs. Their experiences deserve to be heard. Their stories deserve to be memorialized. As a member of the Black UVA community, I felt a unique obligation to take on this project. I see this project also as a love letter to the women of Black UVA.

I also see it as providing important information at this moment in UVA's history. In 2022, UVA's diversity dashboard accounted for Black students consisting of only 6.74% of the undergraduate population, meaning that undergraduate Black women only accounted for around 4.2% of undergraduate students. As I write this introduction in 2024, those statistics and updated ones are nowhere to be found on UVA's website. And the links I had to those data sets no longer work. However, one does not need those statistics to know that Black Students account for a small minority of UVA students. Interestingly, the peak of Black student enrollment at UVA was in the early 1990s at 12% and has continued to decline ever since.[7]

Black students' presence at the university has decreased, but their presence in campus spaces and leadership has increased, according to Black UVA Alumni. During the 2024 Black Alumni Weekend, many were surprised at the number of Black Lawn residents - something they once considered only for White students. A former professor of mine, a White male UVA alum who graduated in the early '90s, even stated how university grounds had a different vibe that matched the more visible Black population at the institution. Thus, the question arises: Is having more Black students in more prominent spaces better than having more in number? Or should the university investigate why fewer Black students now attend? Efforts to answer that question may be complicated by the Supreme Court's 2023 decision to end affirmative action, which determined that the university admissions process must be racially blind. Either way, the material presented contributes to understanding UVA student life and experiences for marginalized communities, especially for potential Black female students interested in UVA or those admitted to attend.

Of course, this book will not end racism. More than reading these narratives is required. This book's contents can be used to understand materials and ways the institution can improve the Black student experience, while also determining who is responsible for implementing those changes. Students have a voice to express their grievances and build community at their discretion. The institution has ears to listen and deep pockets for opening. UVA remains responsible for adequately supporting student cultural programs and offices through funding. The student body is what adds value to the university. Therefore, it is in the institution's best interest and responsibility to listen to and support all students, especially those traditionally marginalized from its community. However, as vocal UVA's student body may be in the spirit of the institution's long held tradition of student governance, university procedure and policy also remain a key place of interest and influence for outside parties.

I believe this research benefits and should inform the practices of UVA institutional offices such as Admissions, the Office of Multicultural Student Affairs, and the Office of African American Affairs, as these are offices integral to the student experience and depiction of UVA. Additionally, it provides insight into the support present to aid Black female students at UVA and encourages the implementation of other supportive systems. These narratives serve as a reminder that although UVA is a PWI, it has a vibrant community of Black students whose presence, work, and experiences enrich campus life for their respective communities and the institution at large. However, UVA alumni and the state government-appointed University Board of Visitors maintain power and sway that oftentimes, and even presently subvert successful student initiatives and expectations.

As of fall 2024, the University has suspended the University Guides Service, a student-led club and organization dedicated to providing admission and historical tours to prospective students and families throughout the year. The university cites the pause on University Guides tours due to an issue of "quality" indicated through admission tour surveys. University Guides student tour guides anecdotally suggest otherwise and note that much of the issues surrounding their tours are related to them acknowledging the University's explicitly interwoven relationship with slavery, which remains reflected in the very architecture of the University as it was built by enslaved people. For example, the "serpentine" garden walls are high because they were constructed to obscure passersby's view of laboring enslaved people.[8] The University's founder, Thomas Jefferson, owned enslaved people and even had children with Sally Hemings, one of the young, enslaved women he owned.[9] These are historically accurate facts, among many others, that are without question relevant to the University and its history as an American institution.

There are Black students admitted to and in attendance at UVA who are descended from enslaved laborers who built the university, one of whom is featured in this book. Therefore, why suppress efforts to educate prospective students and families about the institution's relationship with enslavement, a common relationship found with many American institutions of higher education, especially within the South? While some may find the school's history ugly, in the past, and view acknowledging it as a deterrent to prospective students. I see those efforts to suppress UVA's history for what they are - coordinated attacks from the conservative right to disturb and confiscate educational efforts that highlight the historical and present-day plights of Black and Brown communities. All of this has created an interesting yet stringent relationship between the student body, UVA, the institution, certain factions of the UVA alumni community, and beyond. Therefore, those who read this book should pay special attention to the conversations surrounding the University's investment in Black students and how students view the institution's commitment to diversity and acknowledging its relationship with slavery.

Lastly, this book prompts other individuals to think about their identity and how they conceptualize themselves and unpack how that has changed over time. While also sparking contemplation regarding how one navigates university community building. Who do you seek it with, and why? And lastly, what is the university's role or responsibility for fostering community and support for marginalized individuals? All of these are questions I don't anticipate everyone having all the answers to. I don't even have them all for myself. However, this book provides insight into what Black women at the university make of them and how they've chosen to navigate the institution as a response.

Chapter 1:
Neveah
2nd Year

Part of being a Black woman is just your style, your personal style, how you dress, your hair, your first-time getting braids.

The typical getting your hair done in the kitchen and your grandma smacks you with the plastic comb. Oh, beauty is pain. I was raised on beauty is pain with my hair. The hot comb. Getting burnt by the hot comb, that shaped my experience as a Black woman. I think 8th grade is when my mom let me get acrylic nails for the first time. They were really short, but my mom had crazy nails and all that. Yeah, so I got to do that early on. Most people were like, "My mom did not let me get a set of nails until I was in high school." I was like, "My mom let me do them early." My mom was born in 1981, so she was coming up in the 1990s and stuff like that, so she was a typical early 2000s girl. Stereotypical, literally.So, I got to have a really fun experience with a lot of bougie makeup and nails and hair. It was a lot of hair. It was a lot of beauty. It was also realizing that my hair was different because I was in dance, and it was predominantly White. And then the hairstyles and things they make you do for dance, that was a struggle because my hair wasn't like that. So, my hair was also straightened a lot. My hair is still relaxed, actually. My hair was relaxed all my life because of dance. Mostly because it was a hassle to straighten it.

I was always very outspoken about my Blackness, though. Also, as a Black woman, feeling pressured to fit into the Black body standard, which is thick, figure eight, and that was a thing, and obviously, I wasn't getting enough rice and cabbage. So just that, and just acknowledging that I am Black in a society, especially in Southern Virginia. Before coming to UVA, I was in an area that was evenly distributed by race. A lot of Blackness was around me. Therefore, I had a normal Black woman experience. I don't think there was anything truly significant that was specific to me being a Black woman that happened just to me. Only the typical things that Black women, that Black people, deal with growing up.

In 2020, for instance, when George Floyd happened, I was seventeen years old. I was very active. I organized protests in my small southern conservative town. That was interesting. It was very successful. I think 400 people ended up showing up at the protest. It was really amazing to see that many people from my small town come together and stand for something. And not only that, a lot of the conversations regarding the elections usually tended to spiral into conversations that affect race and gender. And before Roe versus Wade was overturned, two years before all that happened, there were a lot of conversations about abortion. Political conversations always end up somehow getting to abortion. I don't know why, women's rights have forced me to talk about my womanhood and my rights as a woman, my reproductive rights.And there was so much happening with the #MeToo movement. People were coming forward about sexual assaults and sexual violence. I grew up on any social media where we're exposed to so much, where everything is just thrown at us. My whole high school, from freshman to senior year, is when everything was happening. So much happened that really forced me to speak my truth, be proud of who I am, and speak up. Because when I speak up, I'm not just speaking up to say something. I'm speaking up because this is personal. It's a personal issue that affects me. After I organized my first protest, I ended up being a part of organizing three demonstrations around that same time period. And afterward, I honestly stopped. I took a break. I stepped back a lot from social media. It was bad because on TikTok, every time I got on it was political. So, I had to stop using TikTok for a month because it became so depressing. And it's just so much to carry especially when everything feels like a blow to you. If I'm not being hated for being Black, I'm being hated for being a woman. And if not hated for being a woman, I'm hated for almost anything else. It's just a lot that's going on.

My high school was pretty 50/50 Black and White. In my high school there were around four to five Asians, and basically no Middle Eastern students. In dual enrollment and honors classes, it would be the same pool of 10 Black people. So, I would have two other Black people in my class, and sometimes none, because I took a lot of Gifted and Talented classes. So, in classes, it wasn't very even. I would say that Halifax was probably pretty split, too. It was very low income in some areas, and then high income, because. Halifax is Halifax County. There's also a town of Halifax, which is in Halifax County, but my entire county went to one high school. So, when I say Halifax, I'm referring to an entire county of people. So, it wasn't like, "Okay, we have a rich city, and then a poor city", because we really just viewed it as one unit. So, it was very spread out and because of that we had nicer areas and then bad areas. But I do say that probably the average, if not most people, were probably middle class, leaning towards lower-middle class. I'd say I am middle class. See, it's weird. Usually, when you determine your class, it's based on your parents. But my situation is different because my grandparents are in a significantly different tax bracket than my parents. So, because of my grandparents and the fact that they pay for my college, they pay for a lot of things. My grandma is like a third parent to me, and she pays for a lot more than grandparents typically do. I also have a scholarship so they don't pay my tuition, but they pay for college expenses like housing and meals. So, I would say upper they are upper middle class. Whereas my parents make a normal amount.

Coming from where I came from and there being such a small number of people who go to UVA, I really wasn't exposed much to UVA. When it came to applying to schools, I had to see it from two perspectives, an academic perspective and a social perspective. Because all I saw from UVA on a social perspective was August 11th and 12th, 2017, but academically, it's the number one school in Virginia. I live in Virginia, it's the number three public university. I just really focused on that. I really came to UVA blindly. I was aware of August 11th and 12th. I knew that was negative, but I also knew that academically UVA was good for me. So, I didn't visit UVA until I committed. I didn't do any research on UVA. I mean, I went to the website and looked at the dorms and stuff and talked to people who were going there, but I tried to ignore it. I tried to push back any possibility of UVA being this White supremacist hub. I tried to push it back, to the point where my mom was like, "You know what happened here, right?" And I was like, "Yeah, but I don't think Charlottesville is racist. I think that just happened." And I tried to convince myself that

that was the past and that it wouldn't be the present. When the neo-Nazi march happened in 2017, I remember I was in class and it was brought up. I was like, "Damn, definitely not going to UVA." But as time passed I was like, "I haven't heard much else about UVA negative, it should be fine now." I tried to tone that out because I didn't want UVA to be my only option and then I have already convinced myself that I hate it because of August 2017. So, I really tried to push that out and go in it blindly. There's no school that I could go to that hasn't uplifted or contributed to White supremacy or enslavement or any of this stuff. There is no safe spaces unless you go to an HBCU, which has its own drawbacks.

Before attending UVA, well, I really thought that it would just be like high school because I just thought it'd be normal, half people Black, half people White. I've seen the figures, 6% Black, but I didn't think of it. I didn't think I would be able to see the 6%, so I was like, "Okay, it's just going to be like a normal thing." I got to college, and it was a culture shock. Because for the first time in my life, I truly felt like a minority. I feel like a minority in classes. When I came to UVA, I could walk around and count the Black people on one hand. I was like, "No." It was actually scary for me at first. It was scary. I would walk around grounds and every single Black person I saw, I would say, "Hey," because we probably know each other. It really was a culture shock for me. I've only lived in Halifax, so I've never lived in an area that was predominantly White to this extent. It was a shock to be on grounds and really feel different and be isolated. I felt like a minority for the first time. Usually, I understand that there's less of us, but it was different to come here and actually see there's not that many of us at all. I did expect the UVA classroom to be similar to high school, where I'm the only Black girl in the room, which is very true. There are the couple professors that are not very aware, but a lot of the professors, in the smaller classes, tend to be very aware. This is just my experience, but also I take a lot of Politics and Philosophy classes. But my experience is the professors seem to be very aware. They tend to be very open about racial biases and racism and all these different topics. They've made a welcoming environment for me.

I wasn't expecting that, actually. Going to Charlottesville, everybody's like, "August 11th and 12th, racism." So, I'm thinking my professors are going to be racist but everybody was very just aware. I've had a professor go on a whole rant about language and how she wants to make sure the way she phrases things in which she talks about sensitive topics that could affect an ethnic group, she wants to make sure she says it in a way that empowers them. That it's not passive and looks over the violence. That it doesn't victimize them further. I really wasn't expecting that in a UVA classroom. Maybe that's just my lack of educational experience at UVA. Because once I got here, I'm like, "Dang." I mean, of course, you have an occasional one that's a bad egg, but most of them are very accountable to themselves. They really do a lot. I will say that also classroom wise about professor diversity, I mean, realistically I've only had one Black professor so far at UVA, but I had a Hispanic professor, I had a Middle Eastern TA, I had three female professors. I'm glad for that, too, because I also wasn't expecting professor diversity. I was expecting old White men. So that was positive.

I honestly love the college classroom. I wasn't expecting to, but I like college classes. I like the structure. I like discussion sections. I like how, in discussions, we apply a lot of stuff to real life. It's very helpful to be educated in a way that allows you to put your personal experiences into what you learn as well. I enjoy that as well. Most of my classes are pretty fulfilling. There's an occasional class where you're like, "What the heck?" But a lot of times, when I have bad professors, I have really good TAs. It balances itself out. My Economics TA, he's amazing. He is an angel. So, I feel like it's a balance. Sometimes TAs are there because they can understand the student experience more than professors who might be removed. They can understand personal issues better. Really, sometimes TAs pick up this slack of professors who might not be fulfilling my academic and student needs. I feel supported within my academic and classroom experiences. Although, I will say that there is a lack of general support. There's not Black student-specific or Black woman-specific support. For example, with all of the stuff that happened recently with the hate crimes, I had one professor who stepped up and asked, "How can I support Black students in this time?" I also had another professor and I'm like, "Hi, I'm protesting. I won't be in class," She's like, "Tell me how I can support you." So, I've had two professors support me when it came to Black issues. However, I don't know how all my professors will support me until it comes to that time. It's hard to know how they would support me as a Black woman until something happens that hurts me as a Black woman. But I do know, off the top of my head, I know two professors who, well, one that I have now and one that I've had in the past, who would not care. If I was like, "This is an issue affecting the Black community. This is an issue affecting me as a Black woman." They wouldn't care, so it just depends on the professor. And a lot of times, it depends on what they teach or what their beliefs are. But there's at least some people here who will be there and support you.

Existing here in this space, taking up space as a Black woman at the University of Virginia, is itself a big FU to the institution of racism and the institution of slavery and Thomas Jefferson, all of this. As Black people, if we say, "I'm not going to go there because the school has a racist history." We're doing nothing but allowing that racist history to persist and nobody's going to speak up on it, nobody's going to try to make steps to better the university if Black people don't exist here. If we don't exist here, they can ignore us. They can continue to praise Thomas Jefferson and turn a blind eye to all his racism and BS because we're not here. So, I feel like, you know what? It is important for us to occupy these spaces that weren't built for us for that very reason. It's a back and forth. It's a slippery slope. August 11th and 12th is one thing, and the racist history and all that is another. But at the same time, we got to take over these spaces. Reclaiming what our ancestors built.

Every university talks about their diversity. Every university says, "Oh, we're diverse." I saw 6%. I was like, "Y'all not diverse." The funny thing about UVA is when I think about diversity, and this is me as a Black person, it's so binary. It's Black and White. Literally. I get to UVA, I'm like, "Okay, there's no Black people here." I'm like, "But UVA is diverse in other ways." Might not be diverse with Black people. But I see a lot of Asian Americans. I see a lot of international students and people from Asia, different cultures and backgrounds. I see a lot of Middle Eastern students. So, it's like, "Okay, there is more diversity here." See that's the thing, where I'm from, it's usually Black and White. I know there's probably four Asian people in the entire county and 50 Hispanic people, so it's pretty small. So here, that was a good thing about diversity. I got to see people that aren't represented where I'm from, so there is diversity to us in a sense. And it's on me for thinking of diversity as Black and White. That's just what we fall into when we think about racism, we automatically fall into Black and White. We forget the other ethnic and racial groups that can be affected. So, I do give UVA credit for diversity when it comes to outside of Black and White. But also, come on now, Virginia is 20% Black and we got 6% Black people here. That's not diversity. They can do better. They should have some initiative to increase our admissions to university.

Of course, UVA has a lot of ethnic and racial specific groups and organizations, like Black Student Alliance. Okay. It's not specific. Anybody can join it. But those groups are predominantly Black. But when it comes to larger organizations in extracurricular activities, I would say that it's the same one to five Black people, depending on how many. If it's a group of 10, there's two of us. If there's a group of 20, there's four of us. If there's a group of 50, there's five of us. You know what I mean? So, there is still not that many of us. And I would say it's the same when it comes to all races and ethnic backgrounds. Okay, it'll be two Black people, three Asian people and one Hispanic person. That's diverse, but everything's still going to be predominantly White. I mean they're the majority, technically. But, I mean, it's some diversity but not enough diversity. Especially when it comes to powerful positions in organizations on grounds. There could be more done with diversity. A lot of Executive Boards are comprised of White students for a lot of organizations. In most of the organizations I'm in, I'm the only Black person. I'm in Student Council, in the Community Engagements Agency. There are two Black people. I'm in the women's network that just recently started at UVA. There are actually three of us there because I personally recruited the other two to join and be on Exec. I'm in Stitch it to the Patriarchy and I'm the only Black person. I just joined Honor as an advisor. I don't really know about Honor's demographics, but we had a welcome picnic and there were three Black people. I know that that's not all of Honor, but there were three of us. I'm a Legal Clinic Intern at the Women's Center and if you look at our intern class, there are two of us. I mean, we see the diversity or lack thereof.

I had an issue with a roommate before even coming to UVA. I was supposed to have my friend as a roommate. I ended up getting a random roommate. That really threw things off. So, community wise, I was slow. I knew people. We had a Black at UVA group chat for my class. So those are the people I knew. I was thinking, I'm going to be around these people, we're going to have our little group and those are just going to be us. Did not happen. I was expecting my friend group coming to UVA to also be more diverse than it was my first year. I had no White friends at UVA in my first year nor this year, until I met my roommate. And we were barely friends. It's weird to me that I'm at a space where I'm a minority and I'm only friends with Black people. I don't know how that managed to happen. Black people at the university gravitate towards one another, but I had to step back and be like, "Damn, I don't have a single White friend." And my roommate, me and her were cool, but it was like "We're going to live together next year, but we ain't got to be super close." So now it's changed because of her and her friends, who were around me, I consider my friends too. So, I'll go out more with her and be around different crowds of people. I really fell into a protective bubble because I ended up just being around people who looked like me. I think that is bad because you lack different perspectives. And sometimes you lose different experiences at UVA when you're just with the same group of people.

But my community was just Black. That possibly has to do with some other stuff. I feel like I couldn't relate to a lot of White people at UVA. I don't enjoy feeling different in a bad way. Sometimes, as I said earlier, when I talk to my roommate, she talks about Italy or Disney World and it's just culture shock. Of course there's people here who are just normal, everyday people, but a lot of the people here, their life experiences are so different than mine. I can't relate to them. And I think about the boundaries of a friendship where you feel you can't relate to that person or each of your lives were so drastically different. I feel at least with the Black students, there was at least something in common so that everything else that was different among us could probably be gotten over. There would be at least some things that we could relate to with them. And so it was just about comfortability. I felt comfortable being around them because I knew that we shared something in common. I know this isn't a specifically Black thing. It's really a conversation about generational wealth. I feel like the Black community has less generational wealth than White communities. There's a lot of factors that go into that. White people have had longer to establish themselves in this country versus Black people because of enslavement, racism, Jim Crow, and all that prohibited Black people from excelling. I am the first generation to try to continue the generational wealth of my grandparents. But we don't have generational wealth. My grandparents have wealth. It's my job to make it generational. A lot of the White students here they have this generational wealth. Their parents weren't the first person in their family to have wealth. A lot of them aren't first-generation. All their family members went to college. They have all upper-middle class for generations and generations and generations. My roommate has never been to Red Lobster. She's never been to an amusement park. She said, "Oh yeah, my parents were like, either you go to Disney World or you go to Italy." She went to Italy. And to me, I'm like, "Wow." A lot of people are like that. They'll casually say, "I spent the summer in Italy" or whatever. "Oh, me and my family go every year." And I'm like, I'm the first person in my family to go out of the country.

It's not a Black thing, but the generational wealth aspect and our families not having the same opportunities for so long, means that now we're building these opportunities, we're trailblazers. It's like we're the first to do this. That's crazy to me. I always hear people talking like, "Oh my gosh, I can't relate to this." And it's really that, too. I know a lot of other Black people feel similar about that. And going into conversations with non-Black people, it's sometimes scary because this person can sit here and say, "Yeah, I go to Italy every year and my dad has a yacht." And I'm just like, "Oh my God." Amazed. There's a lot of people at UVA who have a lot of wealth and a lot of power. I'm just not used to that because where I'm from, there's not anybody who has just a bunch of wealth and a bunch of power. Some people considered me like that, where I came from, because of my grandparents and we're not even there. They're not even rich. They're not flashy people either at all. Where I'm from, because of my grandparents, people used to think that I was stuck up in elementary school and middle school. Then I got to high school and everybody's like, "Oh, she's chill." Then coming here, my mom was like, "You guys are going to be in culture shock because there's going to be people there who are really rich." And I was like, "Okay." And now, I'm like "Dang, they really are." And it's scary to me. I'm like, "Are they going to judge me for... I don't know." And to White people I'm like, "Are they going to judge my Blackness?" Because most of the White people are coming from the suburban areas of NOVA. I like to say I grew up in the suburbs, but I have experience outside of the suburbs. I have experience in different areas. I wondered will the way I talk, and my life experiences, will all of that clash with them? Am I going to talk to them and feel like I need to tone down my Blackness? Which I never want to do. If I don't feel comfortable around you speaking the way I speak and being the way I am, I don't want to be friends with you. So, it's just finding comfort in people who are like me. Being scared to branch out of that. And I think that's why I only had Black friends.

A surprising number of Black women that I know are really attracted to White men. That's really not my experience. I haven't had much dating experiences with White men, but I've heard a lot of my Black women friends feeling objectified by White men, like they're just checking a box. There's such a small population of Black men. Dating here's hard. I really don't have experience with White men. I don't even know how to approach it. That's scary for me. A lot of people are finding their husband in college. I'm scared. I'm scared of the dating scene here being a Black woman because it's not easy. It's not the same. And a lot of the Black men here are also interested in White women, so it's like, "Do they even like Black women? "Do you see me as a human, or am I just a task or something? Because some people they call you "ebony goddess." But, nope. Back it up. Back it up. My dating experience at UVA is weird. I have tended to find somebody really early on and just stick with that person, so I haven't had much experience in the dating world. For instance, the traditional predominantly White fraternities. You can go to their parties. I've been to three of them. One of the first ones that I went to, I was dancing. And I will say, though, we dance a little different. You know what I mean? So, I was dancing. I was throwing it back a little bit. This White man came up behind me. I'm like, okay. And he comes up behind me. Okay. He's probably like, "I've never seen a girl do this at one of these parties. I'm going to get behind her." He follows me around the whole party. As I move, he follows. He gropes me, touches me inappropriately, to the point where my friend had to drag me out of the party because he was attached to me. And then, at a second party, I was dancing. He was so amazed that I was doing the dance, he taps me on the shoulder. I'm like, "What?" Then he grabbed me and kissed me. So, in the two times that I've been to White frat parties, I've been objectified by White men. I feel like it's because I'm Black. In both contexts it was related to me doing something that was perceived as Black that attracted them. I do think it's a fetish objectification type thing, but it's weird. But that's my experience. I've never actually tried to date. It's not even that I don't date White men; it's just in my social circles I'm usually just around Black men.

Most of the parties I go to are Black parties and have Black fraternity culture. For me, it's been a more positive experience, mostly because everybody looks like me. When the guys approach me, they look like me and they understand the levels of comfortability when dancing on girls at parties and when to approach girls at parties. Not to say that twerking or any of that is a Black thing, but I feel like if a girl is dancing at a Black party, guys know how to approach her. However, at White fraternity parties, that boundary with Black women doesn't exist when it comes to dancing and stuff. It doesn't exist. At the first party when I was twerking, he perceived it as super sexual when in reality, you go to a Black party, people are twerking. Girls with boyfriends are twerking. They're twerking on other girls. It's not necessarily a sexual thing. It's fun. When he started to grope me and do all that, he perceived it as sexual. At a Black party, I can do it comfortably and know that they're going to take it as they take it. It's a dance. We're having fun. I feel like we understand within our community, the boundaries. It's not like, "Oh my god." It's like, "She's dancing, let me get behind her."

Prior to attending UVA, there was so much happening in the world and there's still so much happening in the world that affects me, being both Black and being a woman.

It's been hard. It's been some hard times coming into it so much. Before coming to UVA, I was aware that I was a Black woman. But I was just like, "Oh, that's just who I am." My identity was important to me, but I didn't feel the need to make it such an important aspect to my personality. I'm a Black woman, everybody knows that. But I wasn't standing up and saying, "Well, as a Black woman, I think…" And now? I will happily say, "As a Black woman, I think that…" It wasn't even just UVA, but it was just as time changed and as I got older, with all the stuff that's happening in the world, I feel more comfortable saying, "As a Black woman." I feel comfortable raising my hand to give a Black woman's perspective. And when it's a Black issue, making sure I speak, "Hey, well, I'm a Black woman, this is my perspective." And when it's a women's issue saying, "Hey, I'm Black, and this is my perspective." You know what I mean? Just making sure that I'm heard. Before I just existed. Now I want to make sure that I'm seen and heard. That people understand there's unique qualities about me that can't be found other places. Being a Black woman is such a unique experience. Black men can't understand you. Non-Black women can't understand you. It's just really saying, "Hey, my perspective is different. Hey, my perspective is unique. Hey, we need to be heard. We are in a specific situation. We need to be heard." It is just being very proud of who I am. Before coming here, I was very pro-Black and Blackness, Blackness, Blackness. And then as times change you realize it's not just about Blackness. Now it's about I'm Black, but I'm also a woman. There are layers. Acknowledging I have two perspectives that need to be heard. They're both equally important to how I live my life, how I'm treated, and how I perceive the world around me. Having that acknowledgment and pride in who I am about what it means to bring being Black and what it means to be a woman together. Black people and Black women they're not a monolith. I don't want to say that anything is inherently Black. Being a Black woman, first of all, it's so hard because we have to deal with the aspect of racism. We have to deal with the aspect of sexism.

Being a Black woman is specifically hard because we are by ourselves in our own category. Black men can only relate to us so much. White women can only relate to us so much. So, we're in our own unique category of fighting for ourselves. I feel that's why Black women constantly have to fight for ourselves and be strong. I feel part of being a Black woman is our strength. But I also feel we have a growing culture of Black women who want to live their soft lives, which I love. Being strong and acknowledging your strength while also realizing you can have a soft life. You can have your Black girl luxury. Soft life is when Black women do have this strength, and we have this resilience, but when you just take time to worry about yourself. You take time for self-care. I will say self-care is not as important in the Black community as it should be, which is bad. But you take time for self-care, you spoil yourself, you meditate, you drink your water, you exercise. And exercising is also not as prevalent in the Black community as it should be. I feel, as a Black woman, I constantly feel the need to work, work, work, do things, be strong. I feel acknowledging that you can be strong while also taking time for yourself, slowing down, and realizing you don't have to carry the weight of the world on your shoulders is a defining part of being a Black woman. Realizing you can take a break. You can slow down; you don't have to fight everybody's battles. I honestly feel torn when anything happens in the world. I would say 75% of the things that happen in the world are racist or sexist. It's like I'm fighting two battles all the time. It's just a lot to hold and to carry. I feel we have to take time for ourselves.

Being a Black woman is also about redefining Blackness. When you think about Blackness, a lot of it is really centered around Black males and Black male culture. We are redefining Blackness as to what it means from our perspective and the things that we do that are Black. For example, reclaiming negative aspects of the Black music, like Rap music. Rap is not only for Black people, but there is rap music that is misogynist and objectifies women. So Black women are saying, "Okay, you want to objectify us? No, we're going to reclaim that. We're going to reclaim our sexuality and we're going to make music about our bodies, and about loving our bodies and about doing what we want with our bodies." And Black women, like Megan Thee Stallion, she gets dragged through the mud for reclaiming that strength, calling out the issues that we have in our community. I feel like most of the time the people who are calling out Black issues are Black women. The Black community will sit there. But we're like, "Oh, we can look past our issues because racism, the White people are being mean to us." And I'm like, "No, we still have our issues that we got to solve, too." I feel Black women are the leaders in calling that out. I feel we need to do the work of redefining Blackness and making it a place that's not just acceptable for Black men, but also a space that's acceptable for Black women, a space in which Black women also feel comfortable.

Chapter 2:
Alexis
4th Year

Schooling. K-12. That's a huge part of our lives growing up K-12. Richmond Public School District, at least during my time there, was underfunded.

The children who attend those schools are mainly in high-poverty, low-income areas. So, we didn't really get a lot of resources. I was around mainly Black people. If we did have someone of another ethnicity or race, they were kind of the minority. I pretty much grew up in environments where everyone looked like me. Being in spaces like that shaped who I am in terms of dialect and the ways in which I navigate the world. I was pretty much used to being able to fit into or understand any situation. I didn't ever feel that I didn't belong in a situation, an encounter, or a space.

At first, we were more financially well off when I was younger. As a younger child, I was in pretty good environments, like apartment complexes, pretty safe. Environments where I'm not looking out of the window and seeing bullets flying, places where I can walk to the store and feel safe. Places where I don't feel like I'll be attacked or something will be stolen from me. Just spaces like that where I can feel comfortable just being myself, just moving about in the world. I don't necessarily consider myself in that economic situation anymore because my mom's economic standing kind of went down as time moved on, as I got older. It kind of shifted for me in high school, which I think also shaped the way that I am now. I would describe the economic area I grew up in as low-income. For me, that was never an issue in terms of being able to get food and things like that. But some of the children that I knew, including friends, didn't even know where their next meal would be coming from. It was not a great situation. Some students, even when they went to the school, for some reason, weren't even able to get free or reduced lunch. So, they weren't getting lunch at school. Neither were they having a lunch, dinner, or whatever at home. So yeah, definitely low income. And I would definitely describe my family's economic background as low-income. My mom works for a security company. She's been there for 17 years, and she's getting no benefits. She's comfortable. She enjoys her life. She has friends in the environment in which we live. She's comfortable. I don't think she likes it or dislikes it. It just, this is just what it is. It's not a good thing for my little brother, her, and me. But I'll be gone out of that environment because I'm getting my life together and I hope to be able to change their living situation as well.

The funny thing is I never knew about UVA. I had planned on going to an HBCU, but then once I applied, they told me about the Ridley Scholarship program, and so I interviewed for that. Then I came and saw grounds and I'm like, "It's so beautiful here." Everyone was super nice. Then they told me that I did get the scholarship. So that full ride was everything for me. I would be coming from living in my situation to coming here which definitely played a part in my decision in ultimately choosing UVA. I also grew up in a predominantly Black area. Of course, even within the Black community, there were certain standards that are more glorified. Most people would agree that I have privilege as a light-skinned person. But even being a light-skinned person, you have to have the perfect hair. You have to have the perfect body. And I would say, I used to be kind of chubby. That kind of impacted the ways in which I viewed myself as a Black woman. Plus, your hair, of course. Feeling like you shouldn't love your texture, like you need to have straight hair You have to have the perfect curl pattern. There was this notion that your curls can't be too tight. They need to be looser. I feel like even growing up in a predominantly Black community, there were still things that kind of impacted the way that I viewed myself as a Black woman negatively. But one thing that I always appreciated is just being Black as a collective unit. I feel like that was something that was always valued. It's like, we're Black. We stick together regardless of what! We may argue, we may fight, but whatever we do, at the end of the day, we all are here to stand in for one another. I think that that's something that growing up in the areas in which I did afforded me. A lot of us met in elementary and all pretty much graduated together. Building that sense of community was just really big for me. Finding other Black females who I could connect with, even down to teachers, who I still speak with today. All of my teachers that I've ever had were pretty much Black. I think I've probably had two White teachers. So, it was a shock coming here, where I barely have any Black professors.

In terms of the shift of coming to UVA, initially, I felt like I didn't belong. I felt like I didn't fit in anywhere. It's like being in class where you're one of two or three or four Black people. It was an experience because I feel like there have been times where White students, who are the majority in the class, feel as though their voices are more important than yours. Or it's like the "I speak first, you speak after me" thing. Or "I take charge of this group, you don't." For me, that would never really fly if it's a class that I'm really passionate about. That was kind of a struggle initially because I'm like, "I don't feel like they can really relate to me on the level that other Black females can." I mean other Black females like myself can. Initially, I did not feel comfortable in class at all. I didn't know it was going to be anything like it was. I didn't really want to speak. I just didn't feel like I belonged here. I didn't feel like I fit in with the student body at large. I felt like everything I said has to be perfect or somebody was going to jump down my throat. It was just like even down to the professors, sometimes. This is never with the Black professors that I've had here, but I feel that some of the White professors sometimes wouldn't understand what I was trying to say, especially if I'm speaking on a Black issue. It was kind of like, "Yeah, okay." Like an indifferent type of thing. It also seemed to be common practice for them to exhibit thinking in alignment with, "When I'm speaking on a racial issue, I need to look directly at the Black students." In courses when my professor would be White or non-Black, they would specifically direct attention to Black students or go to Black students when there was a specific race-based topic which can create a culture that promotes the idea that only Black students are required to speak on racial issues. In one of my WGS classes in my second year, we were talking about Harriet Tubman, slavery, and sexual assault against Black women. In all of those instances, there was a tendency, in the large lecture or discussion groups, to constantly look at the Black students to speak on racialized issues. To explain something in regard to Black people to the class, which I don't believe should've been viewed as our duty. I do appreciate that they want to give us the opportunity to tell our own stories and speak on the history of Black folk, but I don't think it's the job of Black people to educate White people on our matters. It's up to them to go out and search for that. They should also be obligated to speak about this issue as opposed to being given the luxury of silence or deflection to a student of color. So, I believe that it was great in certain instances, but sometimes it just felt like "I have to look at you and talk to you about this because you are Black. I don't want you to feel like you are not heard." But at the same time, it's kind of like, are you just doing that because of the situation or is it because you truly want the class to know about our experiences? This practice at times felt more like a call out.

It was kind of hard and a struggle figuring out how to be true to my identity, if that makes sense, in terms of the ways that I speak. If I'm talking to another Black person, I can literally just talk. But sometimes, when I'm talking to a group of, say, White students, I don't want to say I code switch, but it's more like I don't feel comfortable being full self all the time. There are things that I may say that they don't understand. The ways in which I see an issue that someone who's Black would likely understand wouldn't be grasped fully in some instances. That kind of was a struggle. But once I did find the Black community here at UVA, I started being unapologetically Black and not really worrying about how I talk. I also began calling people out who I felt are those types of people who feel like, "I'm more superior than you are." I feel like once I did find that Black community here at UVA and kind of submerged myself in that experience, it was much easier for me to be my full authentic Black self.

There have been many times when I feel like there are people in class who think their voice matters more than mine. I'm referring to some White students specifically. Even this semester in one of my classes, there's me and another Black girl. Everybody else in the class is White. And if we're having discussions and it's like they're not allowing me to speak. For instance, when two people are trying to speak at one time, one goes "Oh, okay. I'm sorry. You can go" When there was a situation where there were two White females talking at the same they, they were both like, "Oh, yeah. Oh, no. You go. You go." But then when there was a situation where it was me and another White student, where we both began talking at the same time, I'm like, "Oh, no. You can go." But she didn't say anything. She just continued to talk over me. That also happened with the other Black girl who was in my class. I noticed that they would do that to her as well. It kind of gave a red flag for me. This is something that needs to be called out. And so, I did. It was my Women and Gender Studies class. I addressed it by saying to the class, "Hey, guys. I think it would be important to allow everybody's voices to be heard instead of just specific voices." I didn't want to really make it a race thing because I didn't want to make it seem like I was making it, "You're racist." But I did want to have everyone know that "Hey, when we're talking, it's like you guys' kind of ignore or gloss over the fact or act like we're speaking. But then when you all are talking, everyone is very courteous, and everyone is very respectful. I just want you all to give us that same respect." It was kind of like that because I called it out two classes later when I saw that it continued to happen. I didn't want to say anything initially because I'm like, "Maybe this just happened." A coincidence. Yeah. But then when it continued to happen, I'm like, "Okay, now. Y'all got to stop".

Honestly, I feel like I was able to speak up because I just feel like I'm always the type of person who tries to be vocal and stand up for myself. Others may not be able to do that for themselves. They may not necessarily have that courage. For me, it gets to a point where it's like, "Okay, the first time, probably not going to say anything." But if it constantly happens, I feel like there's just an urge in me to speak, especially in an institution like this, where I am a minority. I feel like we have to work hard for ourselves. We have to fight for ourselves because no one else is going to do that for us. I feel like women fight for women and Black women fight for Black women. I feel that many times the urgencies of Black women fall under the rug. If there's something that happens on grounds with a Black woman, I feel like there will be mainly Black women in the spaces where there is a need for protests. I would like to see more students of color prioritize the needs of Black women. Even for the Black community as a whole, when we have been doing the protesting stuff about the noose investigation and the Office of African American Affairs (OAAA) vandalism incidents, I feel like I've seen more Black women in those spaces than anyone else. There were also many Black men there but the majority of the crowd has been Black women fighting for the entire Black community. People at the forefront of these protests have been Black women. Also, when we painted over Beta bridge, "We still here," and then someone went and painted over it. I feel like it was the next day. Very disrespectful. This is not to discredit the action and advocacy of other groups of color at UVA but I hope to see a growing number of students advocating for the needs of Black women.

I feel like I've just always been for our community. Anything that I could do. When I was in high school, I was on the Superintendent Student Advisory Cabinet. Our superintendent just happened to be White, but there were other people within his administration who were Black. In those spaces, I would advocate for the Black students, especially at the lower-funded Richmond public schools. So, when I came here, I wanted to look for spaces where I could do something similar. Unfortunately, due to COVID and all the other stuff that was going on, I wasn't necessarily able to do that. I just joined the NAACP for the political action committee to allow me to do that work. So, that's something at UVA where I took the experience I had on the Advisory Cabinet and brought it here. I feel it correlates really well with my identity because I'm literally speaking on behalf of other Black students and talking to them, trying to figure out the things that they would want to change, and what types of messages they would want to put out. So, I think that that has kind of been always a big part of my life. It kind of came to a halt during my first three years, but now it's picking back up. Hopefully, if I do come here for graduate school, I can try to continue that work.

And now, what I think about more, what I hope for in graduate school, is the warm and comforting professors at UVA. We do have amazing professors here regardless of their race. They are understanding in terms of people going through things and giving extensions, things that you may need if you need help with something. My experience has been that they're willing to help you. Yet, I didn't realize how disconnected I would be. I felt like I would be closer with my professors. But I also didn't realize that coming from high school, that those classes there were pretty small compared to the majority of the classes I take at UVA, especially being a psych major. So yeah, just that disconnect was kind of off-putting, a little bit, for me. But as I got into the groove of how college actually works, that just became a normal thing. I'm actually really happy about my experience in the Psychology Department. My professors have been great. Understanding. The advisors for the department have been so helpful because it took me a while to figure out what I wanted to do. Lisa Ishler has been so helpful connecting me with people and helping me figure out what my plan is after UVA. I feel like that's been really good. Bonnie Hagerman, she's the advisor Women and Gender Studies. She's super helpful. I really have no complaints in the area whatsoever.

For the political action committee, even though that's mixed race as well, the main thing that we're fighting for now is the Black community. I'm a part of maybe ax of both cultural and political organizations, though. I'm on X-tasee Dance Crew, which is the first competitive hip-hop dance team here. Even though it's mixed race, the majority of us are Black. So, we have a lot of Black conversations. Our social events, they're very warm and inviting. I don't have to feel like I have to tone myself down in order to fit into those spaces. I'm also on a collegiate All-Star Stomp and Shake cheer team. So, I don't really have time for joining other things other than the NAACP organization that I am a part of. There's this baking club that I'm doing as well. It's really chill. But yeah. So that's pretty much what I do.

When I initially came here, I wanted to join UVA's cheer team, but I don't feel like they are inclusive. I say they aren't inclusive because they require you to know how to have skills like tumbling and stunting which some people, even if they're great cheerleaders aren't able to do since their financial background may have inhibited them from affording gymnastics or cheer teams that required those skills. This seems like a classist issue, even if unintentional. So, the team is not inclusive for me. Although, I still want to cheer. That's why I'm hoping to come back here for graduate school. I want to create a Stomp and Shake Squad. I've been wanting to do that since my first year, but Covid didn't allow for that. Stomp and Shake cheer is mainly present at HBCUs. That's like the primary, main form of cheer that they do. I don't know any HBCU that does All-Star. What Stomp and Shake kind of means to me was a response to the ways in which All-Star cheer didn't allow Black people to express themselves in the fullness of their abilities when it comes to cheer. So, some of the main things that are highlighted in Stomp and Shake cheer are, of course, stomps, and shakes, which are not something that you see in All-Star cheer. The ways in which we use our voices and project our voices, some people would say you sound like a man when you do it. Still, the intensity of the cheer is much different, and it allows for more flexibility in terms of expression, in terms of movement, in terms of the clothing that we wear when we do it, the songs that we use when we dance. Stomp and Shake is an expression of Black joy, honestly. It's the way that we took our power back. In a way, these were things that we were told we should diminish or tone down. No, we're going to actually turn them up a bit.

Honestly, before I came to UVA, I thought it would be much more diverse. I knew it was a PWI, but I didn't realize how much that meant that I wouldn't really see people who looked like me as much as I wanted to. I felt like, "I'll go to a PWI. I'll go and I'll find a bunch of Black students there," because people can go wherever they want. I will say you are able to form a lot of connections here with people who are completely different from you because there are so many people, different races, people from all over the world, really, who come here to go to school. So, I do think in that aspect, the diversity that is here is different than the way that I initially assumed that it would be because growing up in a predominantly Black community, all I knew was Black. So, that's really what I thought about in terms of diversity at UVA. Then, when I got here, I was able to see Asians, Latinx individuals, Palestinians, and just all different types of people. So, I really love that aspect. Then I also like how other marginalized groups at UVA support and respect one another. Like, when we were doing one of our protests for the noose that was hung, there was another organization that was also doing a protest at that time; it was one of the Latinx organizations. They were walking around, marching in protest and then we spoke and then they didn't cut across in front of us, which I feel like was so, so respectful. They went up the stairs and continued, and kind of took a detour. So just that respect and that calm, that fight amongst different marginalized groups here was great in terms of diversity.

At UVA, there's also diversity in terms of gender as well. For me, I'm straight. But gender is fluid here. I feel like people are very open and honest about who they are. Then there are even clubs and things that are dedicated to certain genders or sexualities. I think that that has been a really good thing, especially for people who live in this world that doesn't really value people who don't align with their sex assigned at birth. That's not something that I had initially thought about because that's not something I talked about growing up. But coming in, joining a women and gender studies' class, and just seeing the ways in which people express themselves on grounds in their fullness, I feel like that is something that shifts my mind in ways that I think about gender and sexuality. When it comes to socio-economic diversity, honestly, I didn't really think about it much until I got here. Privilege is a very big thing here. Even though that's not the case for everyone and there's a minority of people who don't come from backgrounds where their parents have money, some students here can just bullshit school and have a job when they get out of here. I don't come from a background like that, and others that I know don't come from a background like that. I think that there's a disconnect there in the ways in which we understand one another, I would say. People also do not understand that they're speaking and living in spaces of privilege. Such as saying things that would be kind of offensive to someone who literally has to work hard for everything they get, and they can literally just float through and still be fine. I think that in terms of socioeconomic status and standing, that's definitely something that isn't talked about a lot. Still, I think it should be because it's very relevant to the students who attend UVA. For instance, say, if there's this club or something that you want to join, there have been situations where certain clubs and organizations have dues that you have to pay. Speaking to people in terms of like, "Oh, you should have it, so that shouldn't be a problem for you." You know what I'm saying. We're not even going to talk about ways in which you can get funding. We're just going to assume you have it because we're UVA and everybody has it. Everybody's rich. Everybody's parents are rich.

In my experience, if I'm being honest, it's been White women who've said stuff like that. Maybe because when I have had conversations, those are mainly the people who I'm in my groups with. Then, there have been instances where White males have said that, too. There was even a time when I had been in a space with other Black students, and that was something that occurred as well, because there are Black students who go here who are also privileged. They don't understand that, yes, you're Black, but you're also privileged. So sometimes, when you're speaking, you can come off as ignoring the fact that you are financially privileged. That sometimes we may not understand things the same way or think the same way in terms of certain financial situations or just life in general because life isn't as easy for people who struggle financially.

In terms of finding my own community, I thought it would be much easier. A lot of that had to do with comfortability and the fact that I had never been away from home. I didn't really know how to live in another space. Making friends wasn't necessarily really ever a problem for me in high school because it was so small. We all knew each other already. It was like everyone just kind of meshed well together. But coming here, there's so many people. It's like you have to be very driven to sustain connections here. I feel like, initially, that wasn't something that I was really doing at first. That was something that was different than my expectations in terms of how easy it would be to mesh into the community that was already here at UVA. I don't feel like I really had friends until my third year, honestly, because, again, things don't really stick that well. I'm not a party girl. I didn't really go out. So, I didn't really meet a lot of friends until third year when I started going out more and just tried to enjoy my last two years with everything dying down from COVID. Three of my closest friends; one, she's Jamaican; the other one is Hispanic and White. Then the other one is Eritrean. I also acquired male friends, which was weird for me because I was never really the type to have male friends. But most of my male friends are Black.

I'm a first-generation student, so I really didn't know what to expect. All that I knew was what you see on TV when people go to college and from the tours. But I just assumed that I would just integrate into this community so well; I would make a whole lot of friends; I would join a whole lot of orgs. That did not happen at all. I would say my first semester was probably one of the loneliest times for me. I didn't really have friends. The one thing that I do appreciate is that I came in already having a community because of my Ridley scholarship program. The people who also got a scholarship from that program, we were a cohort. Yeah. So we all became friends in a way, even if it wasn't like an everyday friend type of thing. It was like, "Oh, when I see you, I know you will speak. We'll have social events together." I was very thankful for that, which really, really, really helped me out with that. I kind of came in with that community. The Ridley Scholarship, specifically mine, which is the Richmond Ridley Scholarship, is for Black students. Basically, they award a Black student this scholarship with outstanding academics. You also had to have community service. I guess an exceptional student. You had to interview for the scholarship. I know for me there were about fifteen other people who interviewed for the same scholarship as me. It's with UVA, but the scholarship fund is from Black alumni. I consider the people from my scholarship group family. The majority of them were Black. Some of them are mixed. Generally, at UVA there have been situations where in certain spaces, some mixed students identify more as Black. Then, in certain spaces, they identify more as White or Asian or whatever the main identity that they normally use. I don't feel great about them not always carrying the torch of being Black. I feel like sometimes it seems like when it's beneficial to claim your Blackness, you're claiming it. I have to claim my Blackness every day, every time I step out of that door, which I love. I would never want to relinquish any part of my Blackness. But I don't know how genuine it feels when in certain instances you're really claiming that Black side of you and you're like, "Fight for the Black people. Fight for me." But then in other spaces, you're like, "I'm not going to really speak on this situation," or "I'm going to denounce kind of that Black side of me in order to navigate the world." I'm not judging, but I'm just saying it doesn't seem as genuine as they would try to portray it, to me.

Being a Black woman for me, I feel like it means living in my fullness and not diminishing or toning down who I am just to fit into spaces that don't value the ways in which Black women navigate the world, honestly. I think that being a feminine Black woman is important to me because I feel like a lot of times society tries to masculinize Black women or try to make us seem like we're super aggressive or we do too much, or we don't really know what's going on. We're just always speaking from emotion. But no. We can be both. We can be advocates for ourselves as well as feminine women who are also soft-spoken or whatever. We can exist as both simultaneously. But we also know how to stand up for ourselves just because that's kind of been the ways in which we've had to live. So yeah. I guess it's living in my fullness and living in my truth. I feel like all Black women should do that based on what that means to them, whatever their truth is in terms of being a Black woman. I feel like that's important. It's important to live in that. My truth just kind of goes back to me loving myself. It really all starts with self-love. So, loving your features, loving your hair, loving the things about you that others might not value. Not trying to change yourself, you know what I'm saying? Not feeling like, "Oh, yeah, my nose is too big." Not feeling like, "Oh, yeah, I'm too curvy." Literally just loving on yourself and I feel like once you love on yourself and you truly understand I'm a Black girl and I'm beautiful, you can exert that energy out into the world, if that makes sense, and love on other people. Love on other Black people, White people, all people.

Chapter 3:
Rofiat
4th Year

I am from Houston, Texas, but ethnically, I am Nigerian.

I grew up in Alief, Texas, a community in Houston that is very diverse. There weren't only Black people but Latino people, Vietnamese people, just people of different races and ethnicities. But, also, not that many White people.

Where I lived, it was very much in the redlining area. We were separated by class. So, most people were in the same class, mostly lower middle class or lower class. I would describe my family as middle class. That was pretty much the predominant thing because it was pretty much zoned to make it the case. So, wherever you were, that's the high school you went to.

Obviously, while growing up, there were racist moments from people who were non-Black. So, I was very aware of racism very early. However, I've always been very firm in my Blackness. It wasn't a thing I really had to question. I felt my parents always made it known that we were Black. The whole talk, "Oh, work twice as hard." The spaces I usually frequented were very welcoming unless it was a non-Black space. I'm Muslim as well. There were a lot of Black people in Muslim spaces (I grew up in a Nigerian Muslim Community). However, I will say that the non-Black Muslims sometimes looked down on Black Muslims often through microaggressions. So prior to 2018, the way I experienced racism was from non-White people was particularly from South Asian people in the Muslim community. I was very hyper-aware that racism did exist, which is kind of sad. Seeing that in the community was kind of sad. But I feel like that's what shaped my experiences in some ways. Being surrounded by Black women consistently has also made me firm in my identity and who I am today.

Before coming to UVA, I knew it was a predominantly White institution, obviously the history of what happened on August 11th and 12,[th] 2017, weighed heavy on my mind. Honestly, I hadn't had that much interaction with White people, so I was a bit apprehensive. But coming here, I won't lie, I very much found the spaces that I wanted to be in and stuck to that. Outside of my classes, I don't really think I interacted with White people that much, honestly. So, I personally never had any experiences. But I have definitely seen stuff happen to some people I know. Here I see more institutional racism than individual-based racism. I've seen how it's affected my classmates and how things are still not being addressed today by UVA.

To me, obviously, UVA, as an institution, is very racist. There's no doubt about that. I'm just seeing how much they surveil their students, monitor their students, and the surveillance culture around it. I'm also a resident advisor. Observing the extent of police involvement in nearly every resident-related scenario can be unsettling. Especially when their presence exacerbates situations, such as during mental health crises. But just the policing culture is very horrible. Especially given the history of policing at UVA specifically and police brutality in general. It's a facade that we're trying to keep people safe. In reality they don't really care about keeping people safe. And then, obviously, with the fact that enslaved people literally built the university and have residential housing on the graves of enslaved people, it's hard not to notice the institutional racism that takes place.

For me, diversity here is a tricky thing. People like to use diversity as a way of like, "Oh we're diverse. Let's just make sure we hit our quota things are going to be good." But not also taking into account their power. So, for me, I don't care if there's a Black person on UVA's board if they are going against what's good for the community, honestly. UVA hired a Black woman on the police for their diversity inclusion. But it's like, "No, we don't want cops. Cops are not the solution." I guess for me, diversity here is a farce. It doesn't really mean anything in the context of institutions because it's just a way for them to be like, "Oh, okay, we did this thing. So, things are fine." When in reality that's not the case. It's not just about representational politics. Once they hit their little benchmarks they are like, "Oh, we have these different races, different ethnicities, people with different religions." That's what they say, but when it comes down to it, they won't support the students that they try to bring to the school. This institution's goal is to make sure that they are maintaining public perception, especially after what happened on August 11th and 12th. When it comes to all racial backgrounds, classes, and sexual identities, I feel like there could always be more done.

I am an RA. My favorite part about my job is meeting the new residents. I really like that part of being an RA. I think it's really nice. However, a hierarchy exists among Residence Life employees. It's very competitive. I don't really like that at all. Basically, people won't say things just so they can make it to the top. They won't critique so they can get those higher positions. Honestly, there are not enough resources for RAs and residents. We are severely overworked and not even paid. You have residents arriving at UVA, each with their own set of challenges, especially during the COVID. Many of them are struggling with health issues, loss of a family member, academic problems and you're often the first person they confide in about their experiences. You try to help them. UVA likes to say that they have a lot of resources like Counseling and Psychological Services (CAPS). But when those resources fail, the residents end up coming back to their RAs. When their association deans aren't doing what they need to do, the burden ends up falling back on the RAs. On paper, I'd say as RAs, we have support, but when it comes down to things, no, because what if something goes wrong? It still ends up on the RAs. We usually have to pick up the pieces. The system is failing and not supporting the students first and foremost and, then, the RA's as well.

At UVA, the burden is on the students to advocate for more support rather than UVA providing what they should. For example, the response to what happened with the noose was very delayed. It required pressure from students for them to release everything. And if people are already stressed or going through things, having to take that additional step might be so much. I'm even thinking about CAPS when it comes to therapy; there are not many Black women there. It would be beneficial if they had more Black female therapists. I know they have the "timely care" thing, which opens the door a lot more. But I think it could be beneficial. I've had one CAPS session, but I didn't like it. I went in for something unrelated to the incident, and she's like, "How do you feel about this? How do you feel about that?" And it wasn't really related to what I came to talk about at all. There were a lot of assumptions being made. She wasn't Black either. It was more, "I see, I understand you." But she didn't. The therapist only said general things that you're supposed to say, like "Oh, I know that this is happening." It was more facts being told. "I know that you go to a predominantly White institution and you're a Black student. This must really affect you. Maybe instead of you having this diagnosis, that is probably what's affecting you." And obviously, it probably can be a combination of both things, but it was kind of a dismissal of what I came to talk about. I ended up leaving the session more stressed out than I came in. I went in for more school-related things and ended up talking about race, which is obviously related to who I am as a person. But it was very kind of a cop-out answer. "Oh, that's why you're going through this stuff." And obviously, duh, I know that, but it was just not helpful at all. I did not like it.

With all of that being said, my scholarship made me want to come to UVA. I did want to go out of state. I didn't know what UVA was until my senior year. I never heard of the school. I wanted to go to University of North Carolina Chapel Hill. My main goal was to attend a large public school without all the stress. I wanted a quality education without the overwhelming pressure. I wasn't prepared for the level of competitiveness or the intensity of the student body. The constant need to apply for everything felt overwhelming. It's like high school all over again, but worse

But then, there was the Posse Foundation scholarship. Obviously I had heard about it pretty early. I was like, this is a great opportunity. I want to do it. Posse is a leadership scholarship organization that basically sends off 10 people from your hometown to colleges out of state, or sometimes in-state, and is basically supposed to act as a support system. When you leave home, you have people to rely on. My Posse consists of nine people. There are definitely people in my Posse that I really connected with. They help me here. Also shout out to the older Posse. Since there are 10 people in each class, it's just like you already have at most 30 people coming in. All those 30 people are doing so many different things on grounds and have so many different identities. Once you meet them, you automatically just get into so many spaces. I really appreciated that. I loved my first year; it was beautiful. When I first came here, I was like, "Wow, this is amazing." I was like, "Wow, this is so cool." And then people just invite you to stuff, and just by then, you started meeting different people in different circles. Again, shout out to Posse for that.

I don't really talk that much in seminars at the beginning. And I was like, there's probably going to be people with very different beliefs than my own. I was a bit intimidated, I can't lie. My first year I only spoke a handful of times". Then, a bit later, probably my second year or third year, I spoke a bit more. By that time, I didn't really feel uncomfortable talking even when my class was predominantly White (which didn't happen often due to my majors, Global Development Studies and African American & African Studies. Both majors provided me the opportunity to connect with my professors more due to the smaller setting.

I got to really talk about things more in-depth. So, my academic experience has been good just because I had a good relationship with my professors. Actually, there was one time when my history professor said the N-word while she read something out loud. It was not needed at all. People did express discomfort, but she's known to do that. So you can't really do anything, especially when they have tenure. My majors and professors truly made my UVA experience. They were incredibly kind and dedicated to their work, and I don't think I would have had the same experience in any other program. Professor Oluadamini Ogunnaike from the Religious Studies Department and David Edmunds from the Global Development Studies Department were particularly supportive pillars during my time there. When it comes to classes, vetting is important! And then, there is vetting. I always ask people who have taken the class, VA grades, Lous List, and Rate My Professor; it takes time, it takes a while. I go through everything, and then, yeah, I see their ratings. I look at their Twitter. If I don't like what they like, I will not be joining their class. And I feel it's very indicative. So, in most of the classes I take, I feel like my professors have at least the same kind of left anti-imperialist abolitionist anti-capitalist political leanings that I have. The red flags come from talking to other people who have taken the class. You'll hear like, "Oh no, this professor, he just talks about it this way, da da da." Or if they grade horribly, obviously, I'm not going to go there for a bad grade. And if they're just not receptive. I feel like I've been very intentional in picking professors who I know care about the things that they're learning and care about their students.

I do want to say that I think the very existence of UVA is horrible. The fact that slave laborers built it. It's not even a school. It's a company. It's a business company. That is very telling. All they want to do is make money. The way that they handled COVID, the way that they pushed people to come back, the way they forced professors to come back and teach in person and not align with other options. The way that they're currently expanding, it's affecting a lot of Charlottesville community members out here. The way that it's raising rent around here, the way that it's affecting the community. Universities in general, especially big universities, are meant for learning; obviously, you're learning, but the goal isn't really to learn. The goal is to make it highly competitive and highly selective and bring people into the capitalist world. And so it's even seeing whatever major you are in, you can easily end up in consulting. Not to say consulting is a bad thing, but it's just one of those things priming you to work in a capital society. And that's something that I strongly want to go against. But obviously, I found my little pockets in spaces away from stuff like that.

Therefore, with everything that's happened, that's still happening. I just try to do my best to be in organizations and try to do things that obviously help the community. Help those who are currently affected by things. That's the way I reconcile it. As I said, as students, we have a lot of privileges. I want us to use that privilege to help people in any way that we can. Even UVA allocating resources, allocating money as much as we can. I think that's very, very important. UVA is loaded, so why not relocate those resources? They have millions. I guess that's how I reconcile being at UVA by creating other spaces and reimagining what's possible outside of this university.

For example, a group on grounds was able to do the COVID Action Now campaign to get UVA to freeze tuition increases during 2021 which was great! For Muslims United, we do a local and sustainable strategy. We basically get two local Charlottesville chefs to cook for us and we raise a bunch of money for them. We give them all the money. It's about $2,000 for each of them which is $4000 total. It's just a way to connect the UVA students with the local Charlottesville community. Because when you're in UVA, it's a bubble. You don't really see what's outside unless you actively go looking for it. So, doing that has been really nice.

I am also active in Muslims United (MU), Student for Justice in Palestine (SJP), and the Environmental Justice Collective (EJC). Muslims United has been my main thing. Muslims United wasn't started until my second year. And it was started mostly due to racism, homophobia, sexism, a lot of isms, I'm not going to lie, in the Muslim Student Association (MSA). Definitely have dealt with that. Just not feeling as welcome because it's South Asian and Arab populations. That's kind of where MU started off. A bit more advocacy and activism. There is also a more abolitionist oriented stance. It's definitely been an experience.

I've gotten to a point where I'm very comfortable with my identity. I've always actively surrounded myself with people who affirmed who I was as a person. Without them, I would hate UVA, in all honesty. Having those organizations, friends, and social support has definitely made this experience that much more valuable. And I've honestly learned so much. The community and the people here at UVA are really amazing. They really made my experience.

Coming to UVA, I didn't imagine being surrounded by Black people. I knew it was a predominantly White institution, but I automatically knew that was not where I really wanted to be. So, when I got here, I just went to all the Black Student Association events, the Organization of African Students events, and any events related to Muslim Student Association. I went to events related to my identity, and I felt like that's how I found my community. So most of the people that I'm around are Black people. But talking to people, I'm realizing, "Okay, yeah, we're both Black, but we grew up in very different environments." It's how people handle money and what they do for summer and breaks. You notice those small little things. It also impacts the way people interact. I mean, even the concept of Black excellence, in a way, that sounds amazing. But when you really go down to it's just rooted in this thing of competitiveness and capitalism. It's the same thing where there's going to be one person reaping the benefits that end up representing the whole community. That does not benefit the community. It's just more of a façade.

I grew up in a community where Black people always surrounded me, and even at home and school, there were always Black people around me. So, it was like, "Oh yeah, I'm a Black woman". It didn't mean everything that comes with it here at UVA, specifically the over-awareness of your race. But to me, being a Black woman, I don't know. I feel like that's a question I haven't really come to a conclusion. I mean, just being me, I just realized the Black identity isn't a monolithic thing. Considering the history of Blackness, I'd say obviously much inequality, a lot of pain, and a lot of hurt. But also recognizing that that's not the whole thing of being a Black woman., I don't know if I could say specific qualities or traits, but I feel like being Black is being me. Literally being myself.

Chapter 4:
Nicole
4th Year

I come from an area that's so diverse. But even within that diversity, I was constantly surrounded by Black people all the time.

I'm from Brooklyn, but I also grew up in Puerto Rico and Jamaica cause that's where my parents are from, and I always spent summers with my grandparents there. I consider myself to be a very cultured person because I went to a majority Black school, but that didn't mean that there weren't other people there. I went to school in the Crown Heights area, which is also known as the Little Caribbean. Growing up in New York meant that so many different people surrounded me, so I wasn't only taking in Caribbean culture; I took in Chinese culture and also different European cultures.

Coming to UVA, I diluted myself. I knew UVA was a PWI. I knew that coming into UVA. I did not think it would be so PWI-ish. I was severely shocked, even beyond the fact that there were fewer Black people. The culture at UVA is so predominantly White. In so many ways, there's almost nothing else but Whiteness. I was a bit shocked by the community here. Where I'm from community is really big. I don't necessarily think that's the case within the UVA setting at all. People here self-segregate, which is fine. But I think it's self-segregating to the point where there's almost no interaction between other cultures. I'm not used to that. I'm all for affinity groups. But in so many ways, I think at UVA that people only hang out with people who are like them. If you're Caribbean, you're only hanging out with Caribbean people. I don't understand that because so many of our cultures are so similar, even though they are so vastly different. What community means here in Charlottesville versus what it might mean in New York or within the Caribbean community versus the African American community and versus the African community is so different, even though we, ourselves, are one larger community. Charlottesville is so inherently White, so I understand that people want to make sure that their culture is being shown. However, I wish that there was more crossover so we could be that much more visible and that much more powerful.

I thought UVA would have professors of color. Not even just specifically like Black professors, just other people of color. That's not the case at all. I believe around maybe 3-4% of university faculty are Black even less, for Latinx. That's so small when you think about how the size of UVA and who we see in positions of power. If I wasn't an African American Studies major, I don't think I would've had a single Black professor in my entire four years here. However, since I double majored specifically in AAS, I've had so many different experiences. I learn so much more when I can connect with people. That's just the human experience.

English departments in higher education across America have curricula centered around Whiteness. At UVA, you have to take a class on pre-17 century literature. And then the 17th century, and the 19th century, in addition to English 3001 and 3002. Every single one of those classes is mainly centered around Whiteness and either American literature or British literature. If you want to take Black literature, that's an elective class. If you want to take Asian American literature, that's an elective class. Latinx literature is an elective class. That frustrates me. Why are these things not considered literature in the sense that they are canon put into the standard? The only Black authors we read in the 3001 and 3002 classes were stereotypical enslaved authors like Phyllis Wheatley, Frederick Douglass, and Harriet Jacobs. Those texts are important, but why are the only times we're reading about Black people when they're enslaved? It frustrates me because there is so much that we can learn from African literature, Asian literature, or Latinx literature. I don't understand why they have to be "otherized."

I was in a class last year that I dropped. It was about British literature. Everything we studied had a relation to colonialism. I was the only Black person in the class. I was like, "Absolutely not." I have curated my college experience to the point where I am able to sit in a class and feel comfortable in it. I purposefully choose classes that relate to Blackness. I'll have Black professors. There'll be other Black students within that class. I love my African American Studies major so much more just because I think people tend to make a monolith of Black people even though we're also different. Going beyond the stretch of the diaspora, just within the United States, my experience as someone from New York is very different from a Black person's experience in California, which is different from a Black person's experience in Texas. There are just so many different ways we can approach it, evaluating their experiences as Black individuals, so I've really enjoyed learning about that.

UVA is an inherently White space down to the structures and the architecture that they put up. A lot of UVA's architecture is like Greco-Roman, which wouldn't be bad if so much of it wasn't used to elevate Whiteness and promote the idea that Whiteness is superior to other people. I don't think the university is committed to diversity in the sense it wants to be. I still do very much think that, in so many ways, diversity is just a checkbox that they can check and say, "Yeah, we have this person." That's sad. If we truly really wanted a sense of diversity at this university, it goes beyond racial identity; you'd have to add socioeconomic background. If you think about it, most people at UVA are rich. Most UVA students are within that top 10 bracket of wealth. Which, if we think about it, that's absurd. Whereas I'm a first-generation, low-income student, which is not what most people are at UVA. I'd probably say maybe 90% of UVA students have money. That's not diverse in any way, sense, or form

I also don't think UVA fosters a sense of inclusion. We need to check ourselves and ask, inclusion for who? Because there's a specific set or group of people who feel included here, who feel seen here, who feel represented, who feel safe and comfortable here. That's not the case for everyone. I always find it ironic when people bring up affirmative action because the biggest group of people who benefited from affirmative action has always been White women. Diversity is much more than race. Like where are our students who are visibly LBGTQ, visibly trans? I think UVA has been stagnant for a very long time. They are making changes but change that's so small that it is almost as if it doesn't really matter. In order to be capable of change, you have to want change. UVA is in need of radical change. The institution could be capable if they truly committed themselves to it, but I don't think they will.

My core community has always been like who I consider myself to be. My closest friends are Caribbean or Latinx. My home base has always been my people, specifically Black people. However, I have White friends, too. My UVA community is a lot more expansive than my community at home because I don't interact with White people as much when I'm home. However, as a Black person, I always knew I wanted to surround myself with people who look like me. Whether that was Black or whether that was Afro Latinx or whether that was Latinx. I wanted to be able to be my entire self within that community. I don't know if I've achieved that at UVA, just because many of those groups are segregated. The Latinx community is Latinx. The Black community is the Black community. In a way, you kind of have to choose. There is very little room to be both, which I think is sad cause I think there are so many similarities between these communities. I have to hop around from community to community. If I'm at OAAA, I'm talking to my Black friends. If I'm in the Latinx Student Center (LSC), I'm talking to my Latinx friends. I'm also a part of the first-generation student community. In a lot of ways, these groups of people don't interact. Not because they can't, but I don't think they have the desire. It's more difficult to build up that larger sense of community even though I have communities here that I fit into.

The Student Organization for Caribbean Awareness, SOCA, is one of my biggest involvements on grounds. I'm also in the Peer Advisor program (PA). I'm on the executive board for that just because I love mentorship and mentoring people. My first year I did the Peer Mentoring Program (PMP), which is kind of like the peer advisor program for Latinx students. I've been in BSA since my first year and was a part of the Cultural Organization for Latin Americans (COLA), which is like the Latinx student organization. I've also volunteered through Madison House. Now that I'm in my fourth year, I was just like, I'm not doing all this stuff. I really dialed it back. Now, I'm trying to spend more time with the people I enjoy as individuals. But I really enjoyed my clubs. I've met so many people. I've learned so much about people's experiences and how your experiences really make you who you are. Outside of school activities, I'm a smaller group gatherer, so I like to host dinner parties. I'll have all my friends come over, I'll cook something, and we'll just hang out then. Or like my friend had a thing, we all went to her house. We ate food, played spades, and danced.

When it comes to dating at UVA, I was talking to someone at one point; it just didn't work out. I don't know if it's me. I will say I do have incredibly high standards. Okay. I can admit that. I know my value. I don't believe in settling. I don't believe in making myself smaller to fit other people into my life. I think that's something that I've learned throughout like my life. I am who I am. I don't think you should complete me; I should not complete you. I think we should be two individuals who create something better. But I don't know what it is with UVA people. I think part of it is because I don't believe many people find me attractive here. I've been told that UVA men like White women. That's just because of the environment that we're in. Even people who say that they don't like White women have a certain idea of what it's attractive within their mind, and it's always leaning towards ethnocentrism. Like, do you have a straighter nose? Do you not have coily hair, but curly hair? Even if they're not attracted to White women, they tend to be more attractive to ambiguous or lighter-skinned women. I've had friends who are so gorgeous and very kind, but because like they're dark skinned, they're not the first choice. The first choice tends to be someone with lighter skin. That's very sad. I think that's also very superficial. However, I do know that some Black women have started dating outside of the Black community. A lot of their experiences are tied to how they were treated by other Black people here or they just happened to like a non-Black person who liked them back.

I've also been told I'm really intimidating. I don't fit their perspective of what they want in a relationship, which is fine. I know myself; I'm very outspoken. People say I'm aggressive. I disagree. I think I'm confident in who I am as a person. I voice my opinion. I don't really care if you agree with my opinion. I don't think that a lot of people like that. And that's fine. I also think it's a very UVA thing because when I'm home, I don't encounter these scenarios. I don't necessarily think it's changed as much as when I got here. However, I am more assertive now than I was before I got here. The one thing that UVA has done for me is it allowed me to be a lot more vocal. I've always been a pretty quiet person. Now I'm a lot more vocal in my opinions. Since the Black community is small in number at the university, it's important to be vocal. I also think I've become more assertive because I've grown up more. I've become more confident in who I am. Because my mom is Black, I've always recognized who I am as a Black woman and how that interacts with the world. To me, being a Black woman means being confident in both my Blackness and my womanhood. It's understanding that I don't have to fit like these ideas of me. Whether that's the idea that as a Black person from New York, I have to be loud, I have to be aggressive. Or as a Black woman, I'm not allowed to be sensual or soft. I can be whatever the hell I want to be. It's understanding that my race and my gender are not separate. They are very much tied to each other. So, I can't view the world simply as a Black person. I can't view the world simply as a woman. I'm both. So much of how I view the world, how I intersect and go about my daily life, is tied to who I am as a person.

Chapter 5:
Gabrielle
3rd Year

My school district in Chesapeake was Hickory Public Schools. It was very, very White.

I'm almost positive it's a Republican region. There were many instances of racism in that area, especially in the school system, that have been swept under the rug, especially with my younger brother. He definitely got into more "trouble" than I did. He was a bit more targeted than I was because I always felt like I should just sit in the corner and be quiet and let things happen. Growing up, I experienced a lot of things that I didn't think I fully understood until looking at it after the fact. It was really hard to make friends because no one really looked like me, understood my hair, or understood other cultural aspects of my identity. It was definitely more exacerbating in middle school, I'd say, because not only was I attending a predominantly White middle school, but I was the only African American person in our gifted program. It was definitely isolating. However, since I was more cognizant of those experiences in middle school, I decided to attend the International Baccalaureate program, which was held at a more diverse school high school in South Norfolk. I lived in middle to upper-middle-class areas from elementary school and middle school. In high school, I attended Oscar Smith High School in Chesapeake, but they call it South Norfolk. That area was lower middle class. There I was able to make more friends of color and Black girlfriends. I needed that. I wanted it. Honestly, it was one of the best decisions I've made. Surrounding myself with other people who look like me made me not feel as isolated. I was understood. I felt like my presence was wanted.

A lot of my ideas about UVA have been shaped by my older cousin, who attended the school. She graduated in the class of '21 as a nursing major. I mean, she told me how it is. She was like, "It is a very Caucasian school, but there are opportunities to find your people with the Black Student Association and all the other Black organizations we have on Grounds." I've definitely taken her advice. I've found a good number of Black friends. Most, if not all, of my friends at the university are Black. Yet she was not wrong about how racist/prejudiced this university can be. Speaking as an RA as well, I do feel that a lot of my residents or residents that I've interacted with don't take me as seriously as some of my White male RA counterparts. Microaggressions are definitely a norm here. I honestly don't think some people realize that they're being micro-aggressive, which is honestly insane to me. For example, I was holding a program for all the residents of Lambeth. It was a little "speed friending program." It was really simple: talk to someone for five minutes, then rotate. The five minutes were up, and I was like, "Okay, everybody rotate." There were at least 40 people in the room. Of course, I had to raise my voice a little bit so everyone could hear me. Then, out of nowhere, I heard this girl say, "Oh my God, she said that so aggressively."

That was kind of crazy because, I mean, there's literally 40 people in this room and I had to raise my voice. I had no intentions of being aggressive. I was literally just telling people the five minutes were up. I don't know. That was definitely really weird to me and it stuck with me for the rest of that program. I even told some of my other RA friends, "Hey, you guys can announce when the fog guns are up because that kind of messed with me." They were like, "Yeah, we understand. That was really weird." I want to say that one of them talked to the girl after the fact, which I do appreciate. But just little things like that, from the stares to the little snide comments, stick with me.

Before coming to UVA, I already knew that there would be a performative-ish definition of diversity on Grounds. I thought that they would definitely use us as tokens. You know how you see those jokes on Twitter like, "Oh gosh, I'm running away from the cameras, so they don't catch me for a 'diversity shot.'" I definitely had that in the back of my mind. (If you go on UVA's website, my cousin actually made it into one.) Last time I checked, UVA was only 6% Black students. When they say, "We are a diverse campus," I'm sure they use the pretty standard definition of diversity, representing several students with different racial backgrounds, different ethnic backgrounds, different religious backgrounds, sexualities, gender identities, socioeconomic statuses, and even countries of origin. They'll have a little picture in the background of a nice little mix of people of different racial identities and gender identities. I feel like it's definitely not really reflective of what we actually see here. So, I did expect it not to be as diverse as they advertise it.

I feel like I have to make my own space here. I've definitely carefully chosen my friends. I choose to surround myself with other Black women primarily and a sprinkling of Black guys because, personally, I don't like having guy friends. But that's just me personally. I don't really acknowledge my socioeconomic status. That might be a part of the privilege that comes with being upper middle class, but I am always aware of my Blackness, especially being a Black woman, and I choose to surround myself with people that make me feel safe.

I had a good idea of what my community would look like here because our class came in during COVID-19. We didn't really have any other choice but to meet people online. I went ahead and started the first group chat. Then, of course, you can only have so many people on Instagram. So, one of my other friends made the GroupMe chat. It's not used as much today, but definitely that summer before we all came, we were blowing that chat out every day. So, I already had a good idea of who I was going to be hanging out with here. I was able to put names to faces.

When me and my friends are out in UVA just being Black and minding our business, it definitely does attract a lot of stares. I can't name a specific instance because it just happens almost all the time. It's like people subconsciously, or maybe consciously, don't want us to take up space here. It also happens if we were heading to The Corner, perhaps. The Corner is a hot spot for that, but even if we were just in a dining hall chatting, catching up, or in a study space, people do have a tendency to either stare or completely ignore your existence, especially in study spaces. I could be studying somewhere, they'll come in, start talking really loud, being a little bit disruptive. I'm like, "Dang, y'all didn't see me studying here?" I don't know; it's either one extreme or the other. They're either hyper-conscious of you or dismissive.

As far as the Black community here, I'd definitely say we stick together. Especially in light of recent events with the Homer statue and the sort of intimidation tactics that have been sprinkled around Grounds, we've definitely been very supportive of each other through this really difficult and scary time. I really appreciate it. The biggest one of the incidents was the noose being placed on the Homer statue. We mobilized after the incident. It seems as if we're always doing something because the university has a tendency to ignore us. We are tired. I participated in the initial get-together where we had to plan how we are going to tackle this problem. We had to plan how we were going to get at least the university to do something about it. We ended up protesting. We also sent out the open letter. I was not surprised by the university's initial lack of response. It was truly disappointing. We sent out that open letter almost a month ago and we just got more details on the situation yesterday. They kept us out of the loop. That caused people to be even more scared.

When it came to organizing for this issue, I had to take a break because it was taxing. I was getting very scared. Initially, I was protesting at the Rotunda. I helped make some of the posters. We were up late making those posters. During the protest, there was a meeting at the Rotunda. President Jim Ryan was there. He ran away from us multiple times. It was honestly insane. He didn't even stop to say, "Hey, what seems to be the problem?" He didn't even pretend that he cares. As far as I know, from the events that I went to, around the time the situation just started, he was running away. I feel like he could have at least released a statement or something. But no, he was ducking us. He was ducking.

One of the biggest organizers on Grounds is definitely Zyahna Bryant for sure. President of the Black Student Association, Amaya Reynolds, and my friend Tyler Busch. Black women are the most active in organizing in the Black community. A lot of the Latinx organizations were pretty good allies to us when that all went down. Big names like the Dissenters, that organization on Grounds. They played a pretty big role in that as well. I do appreciate how when we were organizing the protest initially, we didn't come repping our organizations. We were repping just the Black student body at UVA. I think that helped to amplify our message. It's not just the Black Student Association saying this, it's not just other organizations saying this, we're all scared. While it's not the end yet, there are people really, really, really putting in work. I want to applaud those people because they are really doing that thing.

I am in Alpha Kappa Alpha Sorority, Incorporated. The first historically Black sorority. I've surrounded myself with a lot of beautiful, strong Black women who are going to be doing big things in the future. I'm so excited to see all of them flourish. That goes for anyone in the D9. These people are the future. Black Greek life at UVA, I'd definitely say that it is not the same as the Interfraternity Council (IFC) or the Intersorority Council (ISC). We're more community service-oriented, as opposed to just philanthropic. Sometimes, I get a kick when people lump all of Greek life together. I don't like being lumped together with the other council because, I mean, we're just different. We're not all the same.

I was in IB in high school, so I was prepared for the classroom experience here. But as I already mentioned, I am very introverted, and there are a lot of discussion-based classes. Honestly, talking in class has always been hard for me. I am asking professors for help. It got harder here because you get that sense of imposter syndrome. You're like, "I feel like everybody already knows what's going on. I don't know what's going on. Maybe if I sit back and watch. Maybe I'll figure it out. But if I don't, we'll figure it out maybe or maybe not, later." In my smaller classes, which happen to be my African American Studies courses, it's easier for me to speak. I am a Global Public Health (GPH) major. My UVA classroom experiences met my expectations except for the fact that classmates are a lot more competitive and less likely to help you unless you're friends, which was something I didn't expect. I thought everyone would be a little nicer, but that was not the case, especially in my pre-med courses. Pre-med classes are the trenches. People want to be on top so bad that they will watch other people fall. In the GPH class that I'm currently taking, we're a lot more supportive of each other.

I'm only taking one GPH class this semester, and it's my first semester in the major. From what I've seen, the major is pretty racially diverse. My pre-med classes are also diverse, but there's just a different attitude that people in those classes have. Honestly, I deserve a tap on the wrist because I do not talk to my professors much. I know I need to because I need to get a recommendation from somewhere, but the only times I have really talked to my professors is when I need an extension or have a conflict with an exam. I feel like that is partially my fault. I do think that my professors in smaller classes are a little more cognizant of me as a student, as a Black woman. I'd especially say my Spanish professor, Professor Esther Poveda Moreno. I love her. She's a sweet lady. I appreciate how she incorporates diverse stories into the curriculum. We will read an article in Spanish about the first Black woman elected for Vice President in Columbia.

I've always understood that I will be subjected to not only racism but sexism as well, and maybe hair texturism, perhaps. I always understood that that would be a fact of life, unfortunately. The main difference between then and now is that I'm more cognizant of it here than I ever have been before. I'm more aware that it's happening. I clock it a lot more here than I ever have back at home in the past. I mean, you can even look outside these windows. I'm pretty sure we're the only two Black people on this floor right now. You're always hyper-aware of your identity because you're forced to be because nobody else looks like you. That's everywhere in UVA.

What does it mean to be a Black woman? We are multifaceted individuals, honestly. I truly do believe that we should be able to be whoever we want. Some of us might decide we want to be strong. Others might want to be on the softer side. Honestly, I know we're trying to shy away from the strong Black woman trope, but I mean, we are strong individuals because we have to be sometimes. I still don't even know what it means to be me as a person. I am only 20 years old. I feel weird.

When I think of myself being a Black person, I think that's tied to a lot of the history we've faced, especially in America. I don't want to have my definition of being a Black person in America characterized by struggle and being scared. I don't want that. I would say that is something I think about. It can also mean being triumphant. I mean, look where we are. To me, being a woman is looking real cute sometimes. But being a Black woman specifically, we're trailblazers. Any movement in the United States has been started by us. I can confidently say that I'm proud to be a Black woman. I feel blessed. I feel beautiful. I feel not many could handle the experience we go through, but we do it anyway. I'm just another Black woman claiming space in a predominantly White place. I feel like all of us play a little role in reclaiming space, especially at UVA. We know the history of the institution. As a student, I just do my best.

Chapter 6:
A.D

I don't know how representative I'm going to of Black women since my dad is Black and my mom is Filipino.

That's a different experience that shaped me. Figuring out my Black identity was a struggle and still is. My town was pretty diverse, but pretty segregated in terms of race and socioeconomics. I lived in the suburbs, very close to New York City. Pretty much every parent in my town was a commuter into the city. The city I grew up in was a place that was very proud of its diversity. I remember I would travel to other schools for sports, and they would ask, "Is your school a Black school or a White school?" And we would say, "It's both, it really is;" even though it still was a bit segregated in a lot of ways. It definitely wasn't perfect. You definitely saw a lot of separation, but overall, it's a good town, pretty liberal politically.

I was always in AP and honors classes and in those classes, you could tell what class the AP class was by walking into it and seeing the makeup of the students. I was often the only student of color in my classes. Even though I did have other Black people around me, my activities, classes, and friend groups were mostly with non-Black people. I often felt guilty. I thought, "Why am I the only Black person in my friend group and in this class?" And then with my family, we saw my mom's family a lot more than my dad's family. And when I would see my dad's family, sometimes they would make comments that it essentially meant that I wasn't Black enough.

I still present as Black to pretty much everyone. My earliest racial memory is of summer camp in my town, South Orange Playground Camp, where most of the counselors were Black. I was eight, maybe. The counselor tried to dap me up and I did not know what he was doing. He said, "A.D., you have to know this." And I was, "Why do I have to know that?" He was like, "Because all Black people know how to do this." And I was, "Oh, okay, you know, I'm not fully Black, my mom is not Black." He responded," That doesn't matter. That's what the world sees, so you have to know this." That's very clear socialization, you should know this because you're Black. When it came to my identity as a Black person, my dad did have a conversation with me about how I would be treated. When I first started driving, my dad had a whole conversation with me about "driving while Black" and how the police are gonna treat me differently. He went through the whole routine of putting your hands on the wheel to make sure your hands are visible and to put your license and registration on the dashboard. My parents definitely talked to me and taught me how the world is going to perceive me. I don't really have a choice in that aspect, but at home, I learned more about Filipino culture and tried to learn some words in Tagalog. I had both of those going on at the same time.

I came to UVA hoping to explore the different aspects of my identity. I went to an Office of African American Affairs event and signed up to have a peer advisor. I joined the Filipino Club and another Asian American student organization. I ended up finding out those organizations weren't what I was looking for. So, I joined the Mixed-Race Student Coalition (MRSC). That has been much more successful for me. At those other organizations, I was trying to discover my Black identity or Asian identity. But by virtue of those groups being the Asian American student association or Black student-focused, those people were already involved and very confident in that identity. I felt like I didn't belong exactly. They would make certain references to things, and I would not know what they were talking about. The first general body MRSC meeting we had a conversation about mixed-race family dynamics. I was very surprised because the makeup of that club is as diverse as can be, people who are any mixture possible basically. I was very surprised at how relatable certain things were. For example, when my mom was trying to teach me how to do makeup that was hard because none of her supplies and stuff matched my skin tone, other girls would say "Oh yeah, my mom had no idea what to do with my hair because her hairs stick straight and mine has curls." I was surprised because I finally found what I had been looking for in those other groups. I was surprised to find people in the mixed-race student club had more common experiences with me. That made me identify as Black and identify as Filipino. I don't think I could pick one thing. I would just pick multiracial as an identity. That experience in the MRSC helped me see that that is an identity that's not just a nicer way of saying "other". It's an identity that I can relate to.

When I visited UVA, I knew it was a predominantly White institution, but people would always say "There is diversity if you seek it out." When I first came on a tour, I was like, okay, this is not all White people. I can deal with this. It was past the threshold for me where I wouldn't feel like I was surrounded by only White people. UVA tries to highlight their diversity. They say everything is going great, even when it's not necessarily. But I've been happy with the diversity of the professors, I'd say, which I didn't expect going in. I talked to people explicitly when I was deciding whether to come here and asked them if the professors at UVA were all "old White men." So far, I've had mostly not old White men. Some are old White women. But I've been pleasantly surprised with the diversity of the professors. Especially their willingness to talk about different things and relate the material, especially in social science, to the real world. For example, in Anthropology, the professor talked about decolonizing the discipline. I also had a course focused on the history of Charlottesville and UVA. We went to the Enslaved Laborers Memorial and talked about how the curved walls in the Rotunda Gardens were meant to hide the slaves. So, the course definitely was not hiding UVA's past, and that pleasantly surprised me.

When I think of diversity, I think of racial and ethnic diversity right away. However, there's a lot of different kinds of diversity. Diversity of political thought for example. That's definitely here more than it was in my hometown. Everyone was a pretty strong liberal there, but now I'm seeing new perspectives here. I appreciate socioeconomic diversity. You have people who probably have houses that look like those giant houses on Rugby Road. Then you also have people who came here because they needed that in-state tuition. Diversity includes every different identity and every way that we've invented of separating people. Coming here, I get in-state tuition, thankfully because of a military GI Bill loophole. I could have gone to some crazy expensive private schools that might have sounded more impressive or were tens of thousands of dollars more. But I'm here. I'm happy with that decision. And I was glad to find people here who also shared that experience.

I played Ultimate Frisbee in high school and I played for the national team, so I knew that a lot of my community at UVA would be the Frisbee team. That is part of the reason that I came here since we have a Frisbee team that's pretty good. I thought I would have more community with the people in my classes and I haven't had that yet. I'm only two semesters in, but right now, every single one of my classes this semester has at least a hundred people. I have nearly 400 people in my economics class. Additionally, being in Balz Dobie first dorm, I thought that would be a stronger community and it was for the first couple weeks, then people split off. I'm not very good at making friends in general because I like being alone. During Covid, I didn't reach out to anyone and pretty much stayed in my room. I was chilling and totally fine. My only close friends were the people who were on my high school team because I saw them all the time. Coming in, my family said, "A.D., you can't do this again. You actually have to reach out to people". So I said, "Okay, I'm gonna do it." For the most part, I'm closest with the people I see four or five times a week on the frisbee team. I'm getting closer to the people in the Mixed-race Student Coalition. I also completed a program over winter break with other African American students with Truist Bank through the career center. I was excited because there were Black people in this activity with me, so now I'm gonna keep these friends. Although, I've been so bad about staying in contact with people that the same thing is happening all over again.

Occasionally, for fun, I either find a party or hang out with the Frisbee team. We'll host something. But now, in the Spring semester, we have a tournament every other weekend. Next weekend, we're gonna be going to South Carolina. After spring break, we're gonna go to Texas. However, during the fall semester we definitely go out. As a first year, I don't know where the parties are. My friend and I would walk around and find a frat house that had a party and sneak through the back. I can definitely see how upperclassmen get tired of it. I can understand why people who are not in college or young adults can't deal with the college frat party scene. Hygiene-wise, it is nasty. It's quite gross. Like walls dripping of sweat and moisture. It was not a more than once-a-week kind of event. I just can't keep doing it. There are people who go out from Thursday to Sunday or whatever. Not me.

Although I'm not actively looking for someone, it's been weird navigating the different races dating thing. Most of my friends are White, so they're always talking about, "Oh my gosh, this guy's so hot, and he's just the most basic White man I've ever seen. I didn't date a whole lot in high school, but they were White people and, then, one Asian person. It's a weird balance with the people I see that no one's approaching me. I sometimes think, "What is it about me? Am I just unfriendly, or are you not into Black people?" If you're with all these pretty blonde girls all the time, then that's who people would probably go for. I think that is sort of the standard. Although I did go on one date, afterward, I DMed him. I said, "Hey, you seem nice, but I'm not really looking for anything right now." I was trying to be nice because he wasn't really my type so I also said, "I just wanna be friends". He responded, "I'd be down with a friends-with-benefits type situation for sure". I was confused because where did he get that from? Goodbye to him. I don't know how his mind jumped to that conclusion.

I always understood that I am a Black woman. That's how people see me. That's not something in my control. I also understood that Black people often see me differently because of my other identities and not aligning with certain stereotypical notions of Blackness. I don't listen to music that a lot of Black people listen to. I barely listen to music at all. In a lot of other ways, I don't relate to Black culture necessarily. But Blackness is a lot more complicated than stereotypes and a lot more complicated than what may be the most common experience. Not identifying with common experiences does not make me not Black. I don't have a choice in that sense. Race is a construct. It all is ultimately made up. Identifying as a Black woman means that I have, you know, family that came from Africa more recently, since everyone's ancestors came from Africa. I have family who were slaves. As a Black woman, you have a shared history of common struggles that we all want not to move past but fuels you in a different way. You have certain shared role models and experiences, such as having to fight for your space. I feel that I benefit from what people before us did to pave the way. I wanna keep paving the way. They helped break the ceilings. I need to keep going with that effort. I know I'm not gonna be the first Black woman psychologist, but I can be a role model for younger Black women in future generations.

Chapter 7:
T.N

My experiences are solely from a biracial point of view.

Not to say that it's a complete holistic understanding of what Blackness is necessarily, I just want to say that because I don't necessarily think that my experiences may reflect a general trend or other experiences from Black people who are not biracial, who are fully Black. I would identify myself as a biracial. I think a part of my own unique perspective on identity is being biracial; it's cliche, but you never really feel like you are part of a group or can say that you claim ownership of the Black experience. For me, it was very obvious that I wasn't going to be able to claim the White experience.

I think that once I got to UVA, it was much easier, I guess, to find those connections. And I think those connections became stronger because, growing up, I came from a predominantly White area. But here, what's nice about being at a university, is there are just a lot more people, in general, to talk to. Before UVA, I didn't really participate in what I now understand is Black culture, especially online whereas now I believe that I do. Because I engage more in Black culture online, through music and conversation in real life and with my own family, I think that I better understand some of the experiences I've been through before UVA in terms of racism and discrimination.

Growing up, it was pretty hard to find people who could relate to my experience just generally as a person of color. I had to really seek out those specific relationships and especially relationships with people who were Black because there were literally probably 20 Black people in the entire school. That was detrimental to my growth and understanding of my identity. Not necessarily because I didn't feel like I could be friends with the White people there. It was just overwhelming to know that the majority of people in my area didn't understand fundamentally the things that I went through or how to be sensitive to those experiences. Where I grew up in northern Virginia or NOVA, everyone was filthy-stinking rich. That was the norm. Everybody's really rich. I would say that my family was upper-middle class, but there were people who were big ball, diplomats; very wealthy, very famous athletes who owned homes in my area. People were very, very rich.

In my high school, there were always instances of racially insensitive comments, even microaggressions, not just from students but sometimes from teachers. I used to do theater. I feel like theater is often seen as a place for annoying people, but people who also really search for community. People who are understanding of identity. But because Whiteness permeated every single aspect of my high school, it didn't necessarily matter that people were accepting. I don't think that the White people there even knew what being accepting meant or how to be accepting in a non-detrimental way. My director would just do very racially insensitive things and make certain comments. I think that that also trickled down into the way that students viewed race within that space. There were lots of jokes and slurs that sometimes were thrown around and, not just at me, but at some of my other friends as well. The slurs that they used would be associated with different racial groups. There were some towards Black people and some towards Asian people. I think because a lot of people there only knew whiteness, their experiences with people of color were very minute. It affected me in a way where I felt like I had to conform and assimilate. I didn't really have an outlet to experience Black culture there. However, my mother and my family, in a way that I really can admire now, fostered a connection to my African heritage and also my African American heritage. We would always visit my cousins, my Ghanaian cousins and my cousins who live in Smithfield. In that way, I felt at least somewhat connected to that part of my identity. But because I came from an area where, if you're a person of color, you have to assimilate and take in the White trends. Otherwise, you'd be standing out too much. It was a battle between accepting my heritage. You almost had to keep it hidden and not celebrate it as much until it became cool to celebrate. What I mean by "cool" is more people sometimes use diversity and different experiences to seem more approachable as if they actually accept the people that they say that they're accepting. For example, I would tell my friends, "I went to hang out with my cousins, and we were cooking this food." They were like, "Oh yeah, that's really cool," but I didn't always feel that if I brought them the food, for example, that they would eat it or that they would accept it. They would say that it smells. There are still elements of that here because UVA is predominantly White. Obviously, they're going to do the classic textbook cover when advertising the school. "We need a Black person, a gay person, a person with a disability" on their little pamphlet to show that they're diverse. I still feel some elements of that for sure. But mostly, in the conversations that I have with people here, I would say it hasn't been that way. I knew UVA would be reminiscent of my high school a bit in terms of the majority of people being White. That's what takes up most of the space, whiteness. The other communities were something you had to seek out, but here they were, in reality, bigger than I expected. I wouldn't necessarily say that UVA's diverse, but there are enough groups, and they're strong enough, and big enough that you will find community. I would say I know that there are a lot of people who are very active in the Black community or in the Arab community, too. I have some friends in the Arab community who are always going to events. I think that that relates to strength. I think that there are a lot of diverse people and their communities are pretty active in remaining tightly knit, creating opportunities for engagement with other people in the community, and reinforcing bonds.

I honestly didn't really have that many expectations before coming to UVA. I just wanted to make friends. But, definitely, I knew that I wanted people of color in my friend group, mostly because I think that I needed that level of empathy and communal understanding of an experience that someone has as a person of color. If I wanted to rant to someone about something that happened to me that had to do with my person of color status, I would want to have a friend who was a POC. They would understand me in a way that a White person never would. In many ways, I feel like I have that friend group now. I obviously do have really close White friends, but I have lots of friends of color who I can share these kinds of experiences with and not feel judged or misunderstood.

Coming to UVA, I thought I would maybe find more people who shared my experience of being specifically Black biracial. I thought I would be engaging in more conversations and friendships with people who were Black. I would say that coming here

I have definitely found more friendships with people who are Black and, specifically, Black biracial people. But I also don't think that I probably have taken as many steps as I should have, or as many steps as I may have wanted, to be more immersed in the Black community at UVA. I think partly because I don't necessarily feel like I'm always part of it. I don't want to overstep my boundaries. But I think that mostly has to do with my own development of my identity. I know I have a certain privilege that people who are fully Black don't share. I have to accept that. I don't want to feel like my privilege is invading a space that should be safe. For example, I've been to Black frat parties. I went once. It was pretty fun. But again, I think it's my own mental block. I feel like I'm taking up space when I go because I know that there are people who are Black who are looking for a community specifically catered toward them. But because I'm not fully Black and I have my own unique biracial experience, I wouldn't want to feel like I'm taking that chance away from someone who needs that community. Also, some people see that I am biracial and some people don't. That's definitely a cloud of privilege.

For fun, I just go out with my friends. Sometimes we'll go to some of the bars on the Corner, but it just depends. We'll just go to friends' apartments and stuff. There are just certain places you know that it gets weird. Trin, for example, compared to Boylan. Everybody goes to Boylan. A lot of people go there, but Trin is the best out of all of them, I would say, in terms of how many people go there. There's always a line out the door. But what I've noticed is it's just so White. It doesn't really feel like you necessarily have a place there. Going to a place where you don't really see anybody who looks like you, talks like you, acts like you, or maybe has the same interests is isolating. You would want to go to places where you know the people or you know that the people there have the same interests. Or you can see more people that look like you, that have friends that look like your friends. If you wanted to, you could have a conversation with those people instead of the hoards of people who, if you ask them even a simple question, would just honestly act like you were an insane person.

I think in that sense, there are certain frats that I know that Black women or just women of color in general, you're not going to go there if you're over 120 pounds. You're not going to this frat because they're not going to let you in. They'll make you feel like crap about yourself. There are certain spaces that, I think, just going here long enough and hearing the stories of people maybe older than you or people who have just gone out more, that are welcoming and spaces that aren't. When we're walking by going to someplace else, in my mind, I'm like, "I've been to this bar with my friends for an event" or "My friend had an experience at this frat that wasn't that great." I'm like, "Okay. Noted. Okay, noted." That'll inform my decisions moving forward.

Friendships, I think, have been pretty good. Most people are nice at UVA, at least the people that I've encountered because I'm not a calm person. I feel like everybody I've met and had a chance to interact with has been pretty nice. I haven't had too many problems in terms of friendships. The thing about colleges, though, is that people expect you to be an adult, but really, we're just high schoolers in a bigger arena for the most part. At least for the first two or three years until fourth year, then you really have to get your shit together. For a lot of people, it's still a place for development when it comes to friendship. With romantic relationships, it's different. In terms of friendships and everybody's still finding themselves, it's still a coming-of-age kind of place, which I think doesn't always get recognized because people are like, "Okay, high school's the place to do it. When you're in college, you figure things out, and everything's great." But I think it's just in many ways, an extension of the journey you have in high school. Through some of my friendships, I've realized that that is true.

Romantic relationships have been pretty bad because people are still growing, and dating has changed so much in terms of what's acceptable and not acceptable. Things have gotten so casual to the point where intimacy and a real connection with people have faded. It's harder to find. I think in relation to being a woman and a biracial woman at that, because I seek out friends of color a lot, I would also seek out a partner of color for the same reasons I said before. But it's still hard to find someone with the criteria that I have so I still feel safe and comfortable in a relationship. As a biracial woman, racial identity had a huge effect on dating here. I will say I think the beauty standard here for women in the nicest way possible is stick thin, White, blonde hair. I'm not that, so it's very hard to feel desirable by a big part of the UVA population. Not to say that I'm not attractive to some, but it's just interesting to experience the same ways I felt about dating in high school, but with more people, I guess. I think it's pervasive. I wouldn't go as far as to say it's universal. But with a lot of Black men I have noticed there's just this intense hatred for Black women and almost a disgust with what they look like and what they want out of relationships. They are compared to White women, with White women being more desirable, better looking, wanting "better" things. I personally have not encountered it myself, this is based more on my observations. Just in dialogues with my friends or just people I know who are women of color. They're like, "I feel like they only like White girls. I feel like they only like White people." It's a joke, but it's kind of true because we know that that's the beauty standard. Because the majority's White people, the majority of White guys are going to abide by that beauty standard, and then, I think, it kind of permeates the other communities. I'll add the point that it's the worst dating at UVA. Maybe that's just dating in this timeline in the period of time where we are right now. For me, being a Black woman means being able to appreciate fully and actually feel a part of the heritage that I have. It's accepting my experiences in terms of racism and discrimination as my own. Being able to work through them, knowing that I have a community behind me in terms of family, friends, and people who have gone through similar things. Eventually, I hope it'll mean that I can fully understand my identity and be able to participate in Black culture without as much anxiety. Because that's what I'm interested in in terms of media. That's a big part of what I'm interested in terms of career and general interest.

I think being biracial gives me a very unique perspective of what it means to be a Black woman. And obviously, I would like to acknowledge I do have some White privilege for sure. However, for me, it's just being very aware of what my unique perspective can offer others in terms of educating themselves on saying stupid stuff and passing barriers arising through education. I think career wise, it is important to open up opportunities for my voice and the voice of other Black women to be heard. Nobody will understand gender and race in the very peculiar ways that we do because our understanding has so many layers and nuances. Things that maybe White women would never think about or Black men would never think about, we are going to be there to start those necessary conversations and discussions for solutions that need to be made.

Chapter 8:
Taylor
4th Year

Growing up, I moved around a lot.

My mom is from Fayetteville, North Carolina. My dad is from Panama. I moved over eight times in my life. So, I just say I'm from North Carolina, to be short. I'm not from Fayetteville. I actually never lived there. I didn't do middle school, high school, or anything there. It's just where most of my family's from. I've done all my academic years all over the place. I've been to, what, five schools? Six?

Honestly, prior to UVA, the lack of Black women I saw around me kind of shaped my experience and my own identity. I grew up going to a lot of different private schools. At my private schools, I was often the only Black girl in the entire school. When I was in Ecuador, for example, I was there for two of my parent's military tours, but the latest one was the most impactful. I was there from middle school to my first year of high school. I was the only Black girl. There was maybe another Black girl, but she didn't go to my school. There were two Black girls out of the public and private middle international schools in the city. That means out of about 6,000 people, there were two Black girls. That's crazy.

So, a lot of my identity of what it means to be a Black woman comes from my mother. She was the only example that I saw day to day. I didn't really see that many examples beyond her. Even the television that I watched, I didn't really get positive examples of Black women until I got older and I was in control of my own TikTok and Instagram. I could curate those accounts to see what I wanted to see. But a lot of my identity of what it means to be a Black woman comes from my mom. My mom is college-educated. She's a strong ass woman. She's sensitive but knows how to tell people how it is. She doesn't let anybody walk all over her. She's just so strong in herself and her own identity. I think that's where I've gotten my own strength.

A lot of the time the spaces that I was in, I was held to be the representation of all Black women. It was also on me to take all the stereotypes that people impose on us and defeat those stereotypes. I couldn't just do my best. I had to be the best to show that we're not ghetto. We're not loud. And I'm a loud person; naturally, that's just how I talk. I'm also Caribbean. So, I had to tone down those things that naturally came to me. Those things have nothing to do with race and have nothing to do with the fact that I'm a Black woman. Because of those stereotypes I had to try my best and be the smartest kid in the class because everybody else thought I was stupid. I didn't do anything to deserve that. I was just a kid. I was like any other middle schooler. I saw a lot of comparisons between me and other girls in my grade who do similar things but, of course, are not Black. It was perceived differently when they did it.

Honestly, I'm not shy of being the only Black person in my class. For the majority of my life, I went to predominantly White middle school and high school. I went to a really racist high school. I went to a racist private school. So, I'm used to being the only Black person in my classrooms. I'm used to dealing with stuff where I would say something that's really smart or a great idea, and then someone takes my words and says it's theirs and doesn't give me credit. I'm used to people just always doubting me, not always wanting to listen to what I have to say. That includes getting picked last to partner with during group projects. I expected that to be the same when I got to UVA. It was the case, so I wasn't surprised. It's a good and bad thing. My parents putting me in a situation where I would always be the only Black kid was helpful in the sense that when I got older, I knew how to handle those situations. But, it also, it was a very lonely childhood because of that.

Here at UVA, people try to be much more "woke." There are a lot of microaggressions, and people aren't as open about them. Whenever it gets called out, it's a "Whoa, whoa, whoa" type of thing. It's sad because you expect people here to be better because we're the top-third public university. Racism, to me, is the dumbest thing ever. To go to UVA, to still be racist, and to not recognize that you are racist when there's the internet when there are classes that teach about it here all the time, is dumb. There was a whole fucking rally here in 2017. If that's not a wake-up for you, then I don't know what is. I'm just a little bit surprised at how often racism and microaggressions happen at UVA. I'm also surprised by how the Black community also reacts to it. I feel there are two sides to it.

Racism does happen here, but I also believe that the community that we're in sometimes is a little too hypervigilant to call everything racism. I've taken many classes about protests, especially protest culture at UVA, learning about how things have progressed in terms of the university and what the students in 1975 had to go through versus what we have to go through. There is no comparison. Sometimes, Black UVA tends to act like we're in the 1970s. We're not. We are so far past that. There are no longer just three of us here. There's a multitude. Also, the amount of resources that we have access to now compared to then, there's no comparison. What the students back then had to work with and what they got done is so that we're here now. Sometimes, our community isn't as grateful for that as it always should be. I don't think every little thing that happens here that's bad is a racist thing. I also don't think everything that happens here is something that we need to fight; it has to be a protest.

However, there needs to be more of us in certain spaces, especially the Student Council and the Board of Visitors. There needs to be more Black people. There needs to be more people of color in those places because they're the ones really actually making the decisions for the school. We tend to "rah at the wrong things", especially with Black administrators. Sometimes, as a community, we are very hard on people who are in positions of authority. If you take the time to go into those offices and ask to talk to them, you will understand you don't see half the work that they have been doing to make things better. Interestingly, many student protests back in the 1960s were successful because they had the allyship of their administration. The Black students and the Black administration were together as one. Even if the Black students took the lead, the administration supported them. So, I don't want to think that every Black administrator isn't for us and doesn't want to help.

So, I'm often sitting here thinking, "Where's the disconnect that we're not working with our Black administrators?" Because they're the ones with the seats. They have at least a little bit of a voice in the higher-ups' ears. Or they're actually the higher ups and we don't recognize that. For example, with the Homer statue incident and the protest surrounding investigation transparency from the university, if people actually did their research, they would've known what people were complaining about when they had two administrators go to Jim Ryan's office to discuss the incident with him. They were both Black. People were upset because they didn't recognize that the two people that they actually sent to discuss were the two people in the position that they would send anyway. They didn't send Black people just to talk and calm down the Black people. It was the two people who actually have the position that you're trying to talk to about the incident. They're Black, and we didn't even recognize them. There was a disconnect. They were expecting to see a White person to give them the validation that they were listening. But it was the Black people who actually held that position, who were the ones you are supposed to talk to for those issues. And now they're saying, "They're just sending the Black people to calm us down". No, those are the actual people working there. That's their job.

Diversity at UVA was as I expected. I wasn't surprised because I've grown up in so many predominantly White spaces. I just knew when I got here it would be the self-isolation of groups that experts talk about, but for a reason. We're more comfortable with each other. So, I was surprised by how many Black people were actually here. Coming here and having so many positive experiences with Black people was so nice because my high school was in the redneck butt fuck area of Stafford, Virginia. It was racist as fuck. I couldn't even walk to my car without people with Confederate flags staring me down. I had to get my car parking space moved. That's how racist it was. So I was coming from an area where a lot of the Black people that I encountered at my high school were on some "Uncle Tom" shit, just very uneducated. When I was in high school, a lot of Black Americans didn't know what it meant to be Afro-Latina. They didn't know that you could be Black and speak Spanish. So, coming to UVA and finding my space where I could join clubs with a whole bunch of Afro-Latinas was amazing. Then also meeting people of different cultures. This was more of my Black culture shock because I didn't get that in high school. I was ignorant as fuck when it came to identities other than mine. But learning about Africans and the different cultures. Actually, getting to experience and see the culture first through other people first hand was amazing. I didn't know what the fuck jollof rice and fufu was when I came to college. I remember I went to my first East African Student Association (ESSA) date auction, and they were making so many jokes that went all over my fucking head because I didn't know about jollof rice. They asked whose country had the best jollof rice, and everybody at the event screamed out their country. I'm sitting here confused. So, understanding that and making deeper connections between the African diaspora was powerful for me.

I wasn't expecting to meet and make so many friends within the Latinx community, however. I didn't have that experience. When I was in Ecuador, they were really racist. So, to meet some woke-ass Latinos who know about all the mixing that happened in Latin America, who are aware that the majority of them have Black ancestry, was amazing. It was amazing to come into a space where people are just more socially and culturally aware, and to finally not have to argue the fact that I'm Afro-Latina. I didn't have to go back and forth to prove that my dad speaks Spanish. It was a relief. I feel like I'm finally in a position where I can make a change in my Afro-Latinx community here. I can be that role model and example for other Afro-Latinos who don't have that affirmation. So it's been a beautiful experience of me learning more about my own identity and my own cultures just by being in the Afro-Latinx Student Organization (ALSO). Spreading education is my top goal. I do so many presentations on anti-Blackness, how Africans have been dispersed all throughout Latin America, and how a lot of spaces in Latin America were predominantly Black for a majority of time. Debunking all these theories about Latin America is really satisfying for me. It helps me grow as a person and learn more about my identity while helping others learn more about their identity, too, to learn that y'all are not the "other" actually. So, being able to work here and have those diverse experiences is really beautiful about being here.

I am going to be transparent. I had crippling, really bad self-image growing up and when first coming to UVA. I didn't think I was cute. Not at all. I thought I was ugly for a really long time. The only times that I felt cute was when men were validating me. It wasn't validation the right way. It was sexual validation. The fetishization. That's where I used to get my confidence. Fetishizing my body and my skin. The "You're pretty for a Black girl" comment. I used to get my confidence from that. That's depressing as fuck, but it's real. So, coming here was my awakening. For the first time, I was genuinely starting to feel beautiful. It wasn't until I got into a relationship with another Black person that she helped me kind of realize my beauty in high school. But it didn't really click until I got to UVA. I saw all these other beautiful Black women. Seeing their confidence and beauty, especially the dark-skinned women and other people, recognizing how beautiful and confident and sexy and smart and all these wonderful things these women were, that helped my confidence so much. I realized I was beautiful. Even though we don't look exactly the same, I'm beautiful too. That's where it started to click for me, and I'm actually pretty.

Also getting validation from my community around me. That really helped because I never got that in high school. Those people were mean. It was cattiness from the other Black girls because I came in and I was new. But also because I was Afro-Latina. Everybody was like, "Oh, spicy." People were interested in me, but not for the right reasons. It was because of the Latina stereotypes, "I'm spicy, I'm hot and wild." So, finally coming here and people being educated to not apply those stereotypes to me and just realize who I am as a person, it was really helpful. Also, having a group of friends that are also beautiful ass Black women helped me. Them hyping me up, me hyping them up, that's where much of my confidence came from, too.

I literally didn't have Black friends in high school, so finally getting that here meant a lot to me. I love having friends that uplifted me who were smart, strong, smart as fuck. Seeing that makes me want to be like that, too. Sometimes when I think of shit I've done my first year, I cringe a little bit. It's all part of the process. We're young. I've just grown so much emotionally and spiritually regarding my identity. My confidence has grown significantly. I no longer get my confidence from other people. I finally see it in myself. My ability to work with others has definitely grown a lot since I've been here. My ability to facilitate genuine friendships has grown significantly. It's not just because of me. Again, it's also because the people I surround myself with and my friends have been a huge part of that growth. When I first came to UVA, I wasn't an open person.

I'm just grateful to be here because I am getting my degree from a great ass school which is gonna help me uplift my community and give back. Seeing that there's a strong ass Black community here of determined and driven ass people who are doing the same is amazing. Despite the obstacles we face here, we continue to persevere and continue to bust down every single time. It motivates me. Little by little, UVA is getting better because of the contributions that we're bringing to it, not because of this institution but because we're making the institution and doing it ourselves.

To identify as a Black woman, it means to experience a collective experience that a lot of Black women go through. It's having all these intersectional identities of just being a woman and then also being Black, having all these adversities because you're a woman and because you're Black. My role is to uplift the Black women around me and to also provide safe spaces for them. That's what I do as president of ALSO. I provide that space, and I make sure that any other Afro-Latina knows that she belongs here. She deserves to be here. I'm gonna back you up. Everybody in my organization is also gonna back you up. I do my best as a fourth-year student to uplift underclassmen by sharing all the resources I have with them and connecting them with deans or people I know can help uplift them as well. I feel that's my role in what I can do. Also, because I'm a reporter, I use my platform to try and uplift the Black voices that we have at UVA and the organizations that we're in and spotlight the things that we do because we're the shit here.

Chapter 9:
Jacqueline
3rd Year

If I'm being brutally honest and it's embarrassing to admit, I never thought about my class.

A part of me is middle class, maybe upper middle class at best. I don't know why I didn't think about our economic class, but I just didn't. I never really realized the fact that I've never had an issue getting something that I've wanted, not in any material sense. I do remember my dad telling me in a private conversation when we were going home once, "You realize we are in the 0.1%, not 0.001." Now he's never told me how much he earns. I don't really know. I do think my dad is able to afford stuff that I would want, but he's not really the kind of person to live above his means. But even if we live below our means, we still live in a nice house in a safe neighborhood only fifteen minutes away from downtown Seattle.

My dad grew up on a farm in rural South Carolina. And I think living "below his means" was a tactic to evade racial violence. When my parents were married, they had a beautiful home. It was far away from the city. I remember my dad accidentally set off the alarm. When a cop arrived, he harassed my dad and did not believe that it was his house. With my dad being from rural South Carolina, he believed this could be life or death. It's not a joke. Even in Seattle, there's absolutely police brutality. I'm sure the White cop was "how did this 'Negro' get to be in this big house? This makes no fucking sense." That White resentment is part of the reason that Black Wall Street got burned down. That's why the progress of Black economies was stifled. The lower socioeconomic White people saw Black Wall Street and were resentful. They feel that they're entitled to it as White people.

Looking back and recognizing things, I do think that maybe my socioeconomic status gave me more access to certain things more than other people. I'm not saying that it's fair that I had more access. I don't think it's fair. I punish myself mentally every day for being able to be here. I would never judge someone for their socioeconomic status, whether it's lower or higher than mine. I just hope that for my really good friends, my economic status doesn't really matter. Money should never be a factor in friendship. The quality of the person should be the factor. But if it's a factor for you, then, I don't know. It's not a factor for me. That's why I'm immersed in trying to engage with something that I wasn't even considering before. But people see these differences. They align it with whiteness. I'm oversimplifying, but I think it is a big issue in America. I think that's what's made it hard for me as a Black woman to navigate through the Black spaces.I would also say it was hard growing up because my mom's White and Filipino. My dad is Black.

My parents sent me to a private Catholic school in elementary and middle school that had more color. I am really grateful, but I think there were just some differences. I sound a little different sometimes to people. Most of my mom's best friends, if not all of them, are dark-skinned Black women. So, I would be friends with their daughters who also happened to private Catholic grade schools with a lot of color in them. Their kids would always tease me about sounding White or just acting a certain way. That always frustrated me because I don't know what else to say or do. I don't want it to be ungenuine. I think that fostered some resentment. Throughout grade school and high school, I would be like, "So what?" I realize now that's not the right attitude. There's a way to approach the issue. But as a kid, it's just hard to know how to respond when people are trying to fit you into a certain box.

My dad is from the South. He still talks with a Southern accent. There's no way that people would say that he isn't Black. And I think growing up and hearing his voice made me question my own Blackness. Not that I think of my identity as a woman is secondary, but when I think of my identity, it's as a Black woman. I think Blackness is so much more at the forefront for me. There's a ton of people who just think that I'm just Black. I did my ancestry.com and I'm 40 percent White, 30-something percent Black and 20-something percent Filipino. Not that it actually matters, but people see me and say, "She's Black." People will look at me and not even really know that I'm biracial. I mean right now, I'm pretty pale because I haven't seen the sun in five months. Most of the time, though, people think that I'm racially ambiguous. Maybe it's the Filipino that throw people off. I don't know. People have just been thrown off by me. Finding out that I'm mixed makes it weird for them.

In high school, we read W.E.B. DuBois and learned about double consciousness. That being an African American means being conscious of your race and your nationality at all times. It's about being doubly conscious of both of those identities. That America is only meant for White people. In my high school, it was also talked about as being "mixed" as having more than one ethnic background. I think that really resonated with me. When I was younger, I always felt I had to be one or the other, but I never really fit into either one. I always felt really upset with myself because it's not that I want to be whiter. This is just how I am. I think I've always referenced the idea of double consciousness in the back of my mind, of being Black and also of being White, of being able to exist in both worlds. I think that DuBois helped me better grapple with my own understanding of where I fit because it's hard.

Seattle's also a very White place. It is super White. People are super crunchy. People love to hike. People love to go outdoors. It's super granola. That's not all of Seattle, but I went to a Jesuit high school that was predominantly White. That's where I kind of picked this up. I think the part about me being a Black woman was hard because I would never be invited to dance. I always had to bring a friend from outside of school. It was just sad cause I never got that asked-to-prom experience; the big poster, flowers, some grand gesture in front of your friends that makes you feel special. And I really wanted that in high school. I suppressed how much I wanted it. Honestly, I heard the "n-word" in high school more than I've ever heard it here. I think people back in Seattle would seem really counterintuitive. I think they would be so shocked, especially because they have this intense narrative of what it must be like in the South. They have such limited contact with Black people or women of color. You just don't know any better. That's not okay, but that's just what it was.

I remember after my first year in high school, I interned for a city council member, Larry Gosset. He had been a Black Panther at the University of Washington. He was very grassroots activist-oriented, just super big in the community. A great guy. He definitely sparked my desire to know more about American history. If he heard me say something that was ignorant, inaccurate, or just a regurgitation of some textbook, he would say "That's not accurate." He would put me in a position to see there's inequity even in Seattle. I thought that Seattle was this perfect little bubble, that was protected, that was great, that there was no racism whatsoever. He said, "That's not true. Seattle is super segregated. There is police brutality." He was the one who explained the issue of police brutality to me. It was pivotal for me. It helped me really understand that being Black in America is actually so difficult. It doesn't matter where you are.So, race has never been an afterthought for me. It was always something that was in the forefront of my mind. But I really don't know why racism was not something that ever concerned me. I think maybe it's because I didn't grow up being concerned about racial violence. My parents were very much helicopter parents for a lot of my childhood. My mom is in social work. She's seen child molesters. When I had a babysitter, they ran the sitter through background checks. That definitely shielded me from a lot that would've made me more, not conscious of my race, but more conscious of how I move into space given my race. If that makes sense. So, I never really had any fear about how people would perceive me. People always liked me.

If I really think about it, if I were to attribute why I feel so confident moving into spaces without thinking about my race, it is because I have always imitated my parents. I think obviously you mold yourself in the image of your parents, so I think that definitely had to be a factor. They will walk into a space comfortable. My mom is so bubbly. My dad is a textbook extrovert. He is like "You just got to get in there and take over the room. Let people know you are there." I mean I'll walk into a room full of new people with an open mind, no preconceived notions about what's going to happen. This is especially the case now when I'm getting to the age where I give less and less fucks as time goes. I'm going to say what I have to say, you can like it or not; I'm going to be who I am. You can like it or not. That's not my problem. I think I was more insecure growing up, but I still had that same mentality and attitude. Even if other people didn't see it, or if I didn't see it, other people acknowledged that about me. I think being so willing to put myself out there all the time and just being warm broke a lot of the ice. It broke any tension that might have been there had I not been as extroverted.

I didn't really have any preconceived notions about UVA. I think I might have had some concerns, but that was only when people on the outside would offer their intrusive thoughts. The concerns weren't coming from myself. At home, people were saying I was going to have so much fun in the South. And then coming here, people were like "UVA is not the South." But this is the South. Virginia is the South. You know, the capital of the Confederacy is in Virginia. I think people in NoVa are always trying to escape being from the "South" because they're more northern Virginia. They don't want the associations of being from the South. It's just the funniest thing. I mean my grandma's from South Carolina so I've been to the South a fair number of times in my life. I know what the South can look like. I was like, "Okay, well this is the South."

I came to the point where I was like if it's about someone I care about, I will say something. And if it's something that really offends me, such as the "n-word," I will say something. But if I really don't know if I'm going to see the person again, I've gotten to the point where I realize I'm exerting so much energy for people who don't deserve it. I think I also realized that a lot of what I was saying and spewing to people in high school was kind of regurgitating stuff. I think that people enjoy being antagonistic. I don't want to play into that. They'll bait me to come into an argument about politics or something which is unfair because I don't do anything to provoke it. It's brought to me. I engage, but I don't need to engage. I don't even need to talk about it. I know more than you do anyway. I realize I can be politically involved and not have to be a politics major. And I can also have opinions, use other people's opinions that are different than mine, to construct my understanding of an issue. Help me further my own opinion, you know. But I say that because that's why they were teasing me all the time about being in the South.

At UVA, I think that I've been challenged more to think more about my racial identity for a multitude of reasons. I was really good friends with a girl who's Black. I will call her "Betty." We became friends during my first year. She was cool. She thought I was cool. It was nice to know that there's Black people here. You know what I mean? But this girl, Betty, basically never thought I was Black enough according to her standards. She saw me as some sort of project to help me evolve into this "strong Black woman." She considers herself someone who's very strong in her Blackness. Because she is so strong, she wants to impart her wisdom and her "Blackness" onto girls who maybe grew up in White neighborhoods or didn't grow up in predominantly Black spaces. And I say this with venom in my mouth because I think the problem in the Black community is that if you don't fit this specific mold or have this specific experience that you can share with other Black people, you become discounted the more you don't match that mold. I think it's unfair for everybody because it's really limiting. It confines everyone to this one identity of what you're supposed to believe, who you're supposed to talk to, what Black is supposed to look like. It's hard to even really have much room for your own identity. I realized that being in those Black spaces, specifically with this person, I was never going to be good enough. It also dug up some of those old wounds that I had from being a kid. Never feeling Black enough but knowing that nobody sees me as anything other than Black. You know what I mean?

I don't want to feel I have to be a certain way in order to be accepted by people who are Black. You should just accept me because I'm Black. I shouldn't have to feel you constantly picking apart from my Blackness, particularly when it is more by Black people than by White people at UVA. I think that's really unfortunate. There are very few Black people on this campus that I'm friends with who would be able to understand where I'm coming from because it might make it sound like I've chosen another race. You know what I'm saying? It makes it sound like I've chosen White people over my Black people.

And to be completely honest, it's also because I'm in a White sorority and I love it. These are some of my closest friends. I love these girls. They have offered me a lot of support. I just have never felt so loved. These are girls that I will be friends with forever. I just know that. I've never felt less judged by a group of people. But I hate how people treat me when they find out that I'm in Kappa Kappa Gamma. And it is the people who aren't in Greek life. People who don't know people in Kappa. They'll be, "Oh, you're in Kappa." It's because I don't fit that mold for them. But they don't know what the girls are about. I had never thought about Kappa as a race thing. It's just bizarre to me. I think that I've been more conscious of my race because of the White spaces that I've been involved in at UVA.

I remember the Black fraternity party that Betty ever "brought" me to, where she was the one introducing me and injecting me into the Black spaces. It's when I realized I sorely missed out on due to my connection with White sororities. But she said, "Jackie, please don't embarrass me." What was embarrassing? I don't know. I think people usually love me. I love talking to people. So, I was like, "Why would you say that?" It's that you don't want me to acknowledge that I'm in a White sorority. I'm not going to knock them. I love them. I don't regret any decisions. But it gives me some anxiety.

I felt less confident in certain spaces if I was conscious of being perceived as being "a coon" by people. I remember hearing someone in Newcomb say, "Oh, I heard that girl Jackie's a coon." And I'm like, "Y'all don't even know me." You're saying this because of my being in a White sorority or because I look or don't look a certain way. It's unfortunate. Now I feel I'm not in a comfortable spot to want to get to know people. She wouldn't tell me who it was. Maybe I have an idea, but now I'm thinking, "Okay, well these people who I don't know and who don't know me are saying that. Well, who else in this? Who is saying it? Why is this a conversation? All my best friends back home are women of color. They're girls that I grew up knowing. I don't have anything to prove to anybody, especially any Black person who wants me to try to make me feel like a "coon." I don't have to change. I shouldn't have to change for anybody. None of my friends who are White ask me to change. So why would I change? It's not an act. I find it offensive to put on an act for people to believe I am Black. That's not fair.

I'm a big advocate for growth and second chances. As long as you ask and apologize, you know what I mean? If I bring an issue to someone that they were racially insensitive, that it really offended me, I am trying to help them get better. People can't get better unless you tell them. So, if someone said something that's racially insensitive, I would say it was racially insensitive and give them a second chance. Particularly if it's someone that I care about. It just takes one person to make a difference in someone's life. You know what I mean? I think the hostility between Black and White people is furthered because they feed off each other's energy. I'd like to give people the opportunity to do better, but I also have low expectations. I asked my uncle, who is a clinical psychologist, "Doesn't it hurt you that you give people advice, and they don't listen to you?" He's like, no, he doesn't want to take their autonomy away. It's their life. "I'll give them advice and they don't have to take it." I literally got called exotic in high school, time and time again. I feel I'm desensitized at this point. It doesn't offend me, but I know that it's not something that should be happening. Honestly, I'm happy to be the one to say, "Don't do that." My sorority sisters, though, respect me and my opinions. They don't want to hurt my feelings. They are cognizant of the fact that I am a Black woman. They are very empathetic, as empathetic as they can, to how hard it must be for me in this space to just be happy. I have never had White people be so empathetic about how hard it must be. I thought that it was just one of those things where I carried that weight and went through it without people noticing. I thought I was the only one who really had to think about it, you know?

I remember this fourth-year guy, who's in this White fraternity, we were just talking. He said, "I just want to commend you. I think I've talked with my friends about how hard it must be to navigate through this space, being Black." This is just on some random night. He said, "You just carry it so well. I'm just sorry. how hard it has to be for you sometimes. It's unfair. I want you to know I'm so happy that you're here." I didn't know that there were these negative associations with Kappa until one of my friends texted me afterwards. But they were just very supportive, "I'm here for you." Checking on me. I think that being an American and being in this world of colonial empires and racism galore, I'm never going to forget that I'm Black and I, I never want to. I wish that more people could have positive experiences I have with White people. I understand if you haven't had a positive experience with White people. If you have experienced the oppression of America, maybe you're not even going to try and go down that road. I totally understand. I've been blessed to be able to know these people and have these people know me.

I never also felt more desired here. I went from feeling undesired in high school to feeling fetishized maybe. I also think Betty would very much shit on mixed people. She was not really a big fan of interracial marriage or coupling. She "hates White people." I know that when a neighborhood is getting gentrified when you see Whole Foods coming, some people would say "I hate White people." But she genuinely does. My mother's White. Some of my closest family that I love dearly are White. I would double back if a White guy or someone who even was Black thought I was cute or was talking to me. I would think they were fetishizing my race. It's just really hard. There probably is an underlying publicization and sexualization of Black women in the society as a whole. But I don't think that that means I have to tell myself I'm not attractive or I'm not pretty. That they are only saying this because they want to have sex with me. I think it made me more insecure than I've ever been about my Blackness and about being desirable. I still struggle with that issue. Betty is full Ethiopian. Her parents are immigrants from Ethiopia. So, she's strongly tied to her culture. And do you understand what a privilege it is to have that connection? A direct connection to African culture. You have this connection to your African culture that a lot of African Americans don't have because of slavery in America. And you're judging African Americans for lacking a Black culture? Black culture here is different. It doesn't look the same. We have our own culture. We have our own traditions. It's different. It's Caribbean. It's different African, different people, different African Latins people. It's all there.

When I fill stuff out, I say I'm Black. I'm socially constructed in terms of race, I'm Black. I don't want to knock my Filipino side because I was raised by my mom. For holidays, we had Filipino traditions. I never want to knock that part of myself and only accept the African American part. We started doing my ancestry.com. My stepmom's really big into genealogy. She's getting certified for it and everything. It's also interesting because African Americans have a hard time being able to track their history. I think it actually is very healing in a way to be able to track and trace relatives. To be able to find your roots because it was taken from us. It is a process of healing.

I think it was helpful that Betty and I are not friends anymore. It's hard to hear someone constantly saying all the problems that face Black people. That people fetishize white skin and that's why White women are more desired than dark-skinned or brown-skinned women, that white skin is why they get more privileges in society. I think, historically, that is true, but not anymore. I realize you think that everything I get is because of my part whiteness. That is ridiculous. You know that although that's true to a certain degree historically, people don't just look at me and see a racially ambiguous or Black woman. Everything was so Black and White. But we don't live in a Black and White world. Nothing is ever Black and White. There are shades of gray, you know? I don't need or want to change how I am or who I am. Being genuine is a really big thing to me. I feel when I try to match that image, it just didn't feel right. It didn't feel right. I was trying to put on a show. It felt like a facade. This isn't my cause. It's my life. I don't just look Black, I am Black.

Being a Black woman in Seattle just meant being a girl who had romantic problems. Who would face racial discrimination for the rest of her life. Who would be seen in either aggressive light or sexualized light. I think coming here really emphasized that in my mind. I think I learned a lot about myself. I am Black and I am a woman. People will see that obviously. That doesn't change. It impacts who I am. I'm very spiritual. I think that I have been trying to figure out my Blackness. What I need to do to play into my Blackness or feel more Black. You know what I mean? I want to do what feels right. I'm very intuitive and I think that I know myself. I want to become the best version of myself. I don't want it to be hindered because I'm trying to play into this narrative, whether it's the Black narrative of Blackness or the White narrative of Blackness.

Being Black is so multifaceted. I'm in a class on the history of the South. We were talking about how race is a social construction. It's not a biological fact. The teaching assistant was explaining that when they were bringing slaves from different parts of Africa, they all looked different. They all had different languages. They sounded different. They had different features. Different ethnic dress. Different traditions. Different cultures. But the slave owners kept them all together. I'm seeing how that's playing out now. We need to remember that not all Black people are the same. African Americans are different from Africans. And that's okay. It's when you try to make it seem that there is a certain Blackness, an appearance you have to achieve in order to be considered Black by Black people. You're playing into that whole idea of race being something that's cultivated within you. But it's not. That's the whole point.

In high school, I was kind of known as the outspoken girl. I was always just so comfortable saying my opinion. I would have bigger classes and I would still share my opinion, especially if it was about politics. I never felt shy. Now I'm more shy. I'm worried people are going to think that because they see Kappa stickers. I was in a Jim Crow in America seminar class last semester. There were a few women and men of color. I felt obligated to express an opinion that would prove to them that I'm sturdy in my Blackness if that makes sense. They would say stuff that I don't know if I really agree with. I remember there was this one presentation talking about the necessity for violence for political change and action, for social change. And I'm just not a very violent person. I'm just saying I wouldn't, but it seems that saying that opinion was equivalent, to them, as if I was saying nobody should. I think it's hard still for me sometimes to navigate the classroom space with Black people. It sounds crazy, but it's one of those things where I'm hyper aware about being perceived. I feel one wrong move and they're going to be saying, "There's that 40% White talking." I literally heard that phrase before. It's ironic to me because I just look at things differently. I understand things differently. It's not a better, broader perspective. It's just a different perspective.

I don't want to wear my Blackness like I am putting on a show. I want to be genuine about my Blackness. What Blackness means to me does not have to be what it means for every other Black woman. My Black experience is different than other Black people, who have different experiences from other Black people. I think that's life. No one's experience is the same. I think that's the whole point. I just want to do everything I can to invest in myself and be comfortable in my own skin. It is not something that I can separate from who I am, from my identity. It is who I am as a person. The emotions, the kindness, the compassion, my empathetic nature, my congeniality. I think that's what I've decided about myself. This is who I am. I think that's what people see. I think that people see that I'm Black. They know that I'm Black. They see me as someone who is competent in myself and my choices.

Chapter 10:
Kasey
4th Year

I was born in Columbia, Maryland, but I moved here when I was four, and I've been here since I was four, so I basically grew up in Virginia.

I was used to being the only Black person in class usually. My elementary, middle school, and high school were mainly White. I remember we did a fifth-grade pool party in elementary school. It was the night before our graduation ceremony. My mom was PTA head of the class. She said it wasn't fair that the pool party was the night before graduation because that meant all the Black kids, including me, had to get our hair done beforehand. This meant after the pool party, I'd have to get my hair done again, which took hours. Other non-Black people wouldn't think of that as an inconvenience. I noticed all the White kids just went home and washed their hair, whereas I had to stay up and get my hair done. So, I grew up around White people, knowing that I was Black. My mom's mixed but her family was basically White. My dad's family is Black, but I didn't grow up around a lot of his family. So, I wouldn't say anything really shaped my identity of being Black besides not being White, necessarily. Towards the end of high school, when Trump got elected, I started being like, "Well, he doesn't like Black people." That made me realize that being Black was more a part of my identity than I thought.

I'd describe my family and upbringing as solidly middle class. My neighborhood was considered a nice neighborhood compared to the other neighborhood, which was just regular middle class. I was always like, "Oh." Feeling I'm the shit because I'm from the nicer houses or whatever." Not that the other neighborhood wasn't nice, it was a solid middle class but people from there were like, "Oh, you live in the newer houses." When I got to high school, we pulled from a larger area and they had this neighborhood, Salisbury, which has super nice houses. Then I was like, "Well shit, now I'm just one of the regular kids." Most of the time, it was normal for kids to get cars when they turned 16. Most of everyone's parents paid for everything until their kids got little high school jobs, but they weren't for survival, only for them to have pocket change. When I got to high school, there were definitely kids that I noticed had maybe less nicer things than other people.My high school was set up in a way where if you were in the Honors or upper-level classes, you could tell there was a racial difference. If you were in the C-level classes where there'd be a lot more diversity, but then you'd get to the Honors AP classes, and it'd just be White kids everywhere.

I didn't really think at all that my race would really have any impact on my experience at UVA. Looking back, now that I'm a fourth year, I could definitely see that I was "whitewashed" to the point where race just wasn't even a factor for me. Back then I thought that I would've experienced every space as any other person would. But when I did get here, I noticed just from the beginning that I felt off in maybe the spaces I was around. I joined a sorority my first year and I rushed the Inter Sorority Council, which is traditional Greek life. And I was like, "Yeah, it'll be fun." I always wanted to be in a sorority, and I was definitely a little bit nervous about rushing while being Black, but I felt like I'd fit in more in the Inter-Sorority Council (ISC) than if I were to rush National Panhellenic.

However, last year I realized, "Well, fuck this is not it." My experience wasn't the experience that everyone else was having. It just felt like everything was made for them and not me. For me, it was weird to walk into a frat house and there's all these White guys and just the dynamics of it all. I'm in Alpha Chi Omega. When I rushed that sorority, I liked it because it seemed like the most diverse one, which I would say it is. It also seems to me it's its own little bubble of just oblivion where you don't really talk about the fact that every single person at frats is White. That sticks out to me. But for the other girls it just seems like it's normal. So, I felt out of place more there just because the whole culture seems so privileged and so oblivious to other struggles. I started to realize that my identity as a Black woman really didn't sync up to the social aspect of Greek life here. I felt out of place a lot. I came in here thinking just my identity wasn't necessarily that big of a factor and wouldn't really change how I experienced college. Now I'm about to graduate and I really feel like I missed out on settings or situations that I could have been a part of had I really tried to connect more with my identity and been involved more in the Black Student Association and other similar organizations and events.

I lived in my sorority house last year and there were 12 other girls living there too. I was the only Black girl living in the house. It was fine. I didn't feel isolated because of my identity. But at the end of the year last semester, there was an issue. I'd gotten a package from Princess Polly and so had another girl in the house. I grabbed both of them because I thought they were both mine. So I had her clothes and was going to try them. They were all dresses that I had looked at buying and I ended up buying seven dresses, so I wasn't really paying attention to which seven they were. I just thought all the dresses were mine. I tried on the dresses that were hers too, not knowing that they were hers. And I was like, "Oh, I don't like them." So, I was going to return them." Before I did that, she found them in my room. She had gone in my room and accused me of stealing them from her. I was like, "What the fuck? No, I didn't, these are mine." Then I realized they were hers and I was like, "Oh fuck, you're right." But she was so adamant that I was stealing from her instead.

While I wasn't necessarily close with this girl to start, I always felt like maybe if it had been someone else in the house, then they would've gotten the benefit of the doubt. She would've been, "Hey, I noticed these dresses. Did you buy these because I'm missing a package." Instead, she said, "You fucking stole these dresses from me. That's so dishonest." And meanwhile I was like, "You literally went in my room and looked through my things." She didn't understand that going into my room was an invasion of my privacy. I don't understand why she wouldn't just ask me because even if we're not best friends we still live together. I feel like living together you have some respect or level of bonding where you would at least respect someone enough to not go through their stuff. Instead she was so adamant that I was stealing from her. I can't really tell if she was being racist or if she was being biased. It's just little things like that; wondering if things happen because I'm Black or is it a normal response? I did bring it up to the diversity, equity, and inclusion girl. The response was saying something during our chapter meeting, but it was a very quick and brief, "Let's make sure not to jump to conclusions about people and make sure you give people the benefit of the doubt and stuff."

Another situation that happened was during Covid, during the Black Lives Matter movement, that happened while we were in lockdown, but still at school. It was hard to talk about it in my sorority. We have a DEI chair, but I was kind of disappointed by the lack of their communication with the chapter about BLM and adjacent things. We'd go to chapter and they do their regular announcements, but not really bring up George Floyd and the news. They never talked about it. They would just dance around the topic by saying "to make sure you're treating everyone the same and don't be biased." When rush time came around too, I also felt they should've said something. Again, I also questioned myself, like, "Well maybe they don't feel comfortable doing it because they're White." Yet at the same time, it feels like in my sorority, there are things that stand out to me, that I notice. I wonder if everyone else notices or if I'm just noticing it because I'm Black. I feel like my sorority has never taken a hard stand against microaggressions or racism. I feel like they're trying to balance between not explicitly saying what they condone but also not being "bad people." However, I do like my sorority, I like our philanthropy. It's supporting women in domestic abuse prevention. And our motto is "Real Strong Women," which I like. That's very much my thing, being an independent woman. I feel like I chose the best sorority in the ISC but I do wish I had rushed the Divine Nine because I just feel like I would've done so much more socially and also developed as more of a person. I feel like I missed out on that. I was very naive rushing ISC. If I had to do it all over again, I would've done The Divine Nine.

I knew that I wanted to rush so I was very happy to get into Greek life. And I guess I did have that experience. And I guess with the way the pandemic worked out with my member class in my sorority, we didn't really get to do as much bonding. I was assuming that my sorority was going to be my main social agenda, that would be what my social life was based around. My experience was completely different. I didn't really make friends with any of the girls in my sorority. I wasn't really able to play in a lot of girly drama gossip stuff because I don't really enjoy drama. I'm more the type of person that will be, "If this is happening, we need to do this so that I can move on." Whereas other people would just be like, "I want to talk behind your back about it forever and not do anything about it." And just petty stuff, which I didn't really enjoy. The level of community has very much disappointed me. I feel like I'm not really living beyond the sorority bubble.

I don't really have a community here just because I felt so unexcited by the Greek life community that was presented to me. I was disappointed by it. Whereas I imagine if I were maybe rushed a Black sorority, I would've probably made better friends. I don't have any friends outside of Greek life. I honestly don't have friends here at all, which sounds really fucking sad but the only opportunity to make them was between school and social events. Social opportunities always included partying and drinking. It felt like there maybe wasn't really that much time to make actual genuine connections with girls just because it's hard to do that and party. I know that there was somewhere where I could've fit in more, maybe. Maybe it's too late now, which I know it isn't, but I just feel like at this point I just want to get out of college. I have a few friends that I've made through my sorority that are great. My friend group is four White people, two Black people, including myself. My friend group is mostly White. But they're cool, they're awesome. I feel like I picked the girls in my sorority that are not feeding into all the sorority bullshit. We're able to recognize things and be like, "This is fucking weird." My roommate who's also in the same sorority as me, she's mixed. So we definitely have those moments where we're both like, "This is some fucked up shit." I'm happy that I was able to find girls that do see through all the fake sorority BS that there is.

I got into hook-up culture, which is just not it. The people that I have been involved with intimately, I always felt like I was being tokenized. They'd often say, "Oh, I've never hooked up with a Black girl before." Hooking up felt more of an experience maybe for someone else, than it was for me. All of my hookups were mainly White and just one-night occurrences. Because of my social setting in Greek life, it makes sense that those were the people that I was involved with but it was not good, so I stopped. I was like, "It's the same thing every time." I'm not satisfied or happy with the interaction. I don't like the feeling. It was just an experienced type of thing, so I gave up on that part. Hookup culture feels more of a night at a frat. It all seems to be very ritualistic in that you pregame with your friends, you get all dressed up, you go, you dance, you find someone you think is cute, you make out with them, you hook-up the next day, you talk about with your friends. Some people can do that and it's fun and stuff, but other people that are shy wake up regretting it. I did date a South Asian guy who was Pakistani. I'm not going to lie, he was a dick. There was one time where he literally grabbed all the fat on my stomach and he was like, "Does this make you uncomfortable?" I was just like, "He's not a good person." It's funny looking back now. I'm also a super shy person and I don't like talking to boys like that. I always said that I wanted to date in college, but I'm way too fucking shy and I just never made those good connections.

I came in as a pre-med student, so my classroom expectations were big lectures. Go in, listen to the lectures, and leave. I didn't really think there was a social aspect to the classes. After I started taking smaller, more discussion based classes, like Sociology, I found I enjoyed those a lot more because discussion is just your opinions or maybe your experiences. It wasn't what I was expecting at all because I was planning on being pre-med, where you talk about cells and biology. When I was in those classes it was very dry. It was more of trying to stay awake for those 50-minute lectures. Whereas I think that my sociology classes that I'm in, I'm excited to do the readings. My professors talk about relevant things that are happening. For example, I took two classes with Professor Ian Mullins. The day when the noose was found on Grounds, we spent both classes talking about it. Professor Mullins is awesome. I really like him. He's a White man, but I feel like he is very aware of that. He's the most progressive person I've ever met. I really appreciated us talking about the noose incident. It feels like, because the class is *Sociology of Ignorance*, the conversation was coming from a good place to start with because you're talking about people's ignorance on college campuses and how some students experience these situations differently than others. It felt like a conversation with friends. It was less formal than I expected a classroom conversation to be, which I appreciated. No one was necessarily worried about saying the wrong thing or not sounding smart, which I feel like in a lot of the classes when I was pre-med. Which is why I didn't want to talk. I was like "I'm going to sound like an idiot." Whereas I feel very encouraged by my sociology classes to speak. Sociology, in general, as a major very much facilitates conversation.

My classes really have helped me develop more as a person because I'm thinking and learning about things that I just had never thought about. A lot of the reading that I'll do for my classes will be about something that I've been thinking, but I didn't know it was actually a thing that people realized. Some of those readings reaffirmed how I was feeling or my experiences The readings demonstrated that there's scholarship behind these experiences. So I definitely do feel many courses here have supported my identity. For example, during my second year during the pandemic, while I was still pre-med, I took my first sociology classes, Criminology. We learned a lot about the history of policing in America and the prison industrial complex. That class made me realize, "This is the stuff I want to learn about. This is what I want to hear. This relates to what is going on, present day. It really helps." It makes me more invested about the things that go on in our society because I'm more aware of them. It's been a learning process for me, being here, just about myself and how I fit in to the world. My classes have really helped me do that. I definitely wouldn't have gotten that experience had I stayed pre-med.

Before coming to UVA I knew that there were different clubs that really promote people's identities. However, you have to seek them out, which I was a little surprised about, coming in. It's not an experience readily provided as much I would've thought. If you were to look at UVA academic life, these things are there but they're so small you would only look for them if that's what you were looking for. It's not really presented to all students. UVA does do a good job of having these clubs available but you have to look for them so I feel the options are there but they might not be presented on the top shelf.

I think that everyone at UVA wants to make everyone feel welcomed, but they're not necessarily going to take action. It's like, "Oh everyone's welcome here. You're welcome to these classes, you can take these classes." But then you get there and it's not that diverse. I feel like it has to do with more of the fact that, in actuality, students don't feel as welcomed. It's one thing where they say they're diverse, but it's not that much of an actual effort to diversify. Because anyone can apply here. Anyone can go to UVA. But this school isn't really that diverse in terms of class and race. I wonder a lot why that is. Is it because more White people apply here? Is it because the students that meet the criteria to get into UVA come from higher backgrounds because they were able to get test prep tutor stuff that made them able to succeed? Or is it because people generally don't feel welcomed here? I'm not really sure. I expected everyone to be a majority White. I knew that a lot of stereotypically rich snotty kids went there, but I also knew that they can't all be rich snotty kids. I was not surprised by the lack of diversity here. I was more surprised by the amount of money that kids have, maybe the class differences. So, I expected it to be snotty rich kids but I don't think I really knew what a snotty rich kid actually was. I remember getting here my first year and learning about Golden Goose sneakers that were like $500 for a pair of tennis shoes that look dirty. They're already dirty tennis shoes that you buy. I see them all the time here. I also see people with LuluLemon everything. It's also the way that people talk about vacations or what they do so easily that I was like, "What the fuck?" You see people on social media, you see what they do on the weekends. They're always going out and I'm like, "How the fuck do they pay for that?" It's just their normal. I knew people like that existed but it's still a big culture shock for me.

Since being at UVA, everything that's happened has shaped my identity against those around me, more so than I expected. I still feel like in Greek life circles, I am still the other. Perhaps I was denying that when I was like, "Oh yeah, I can be in hookup culture, that's fun." "Yeah, I can go party every night and go to frats and stuff and feel welcomed." Whereas now I realize that I didn't feel like that. Now I'm like, I don't feel like that for a reason. It's because of who I am. Those experiences don't provide the same amount of fulfillment for me as does for others. That shift in thinking came because I'm more aware of my identity and how I'm represented in certain spaces. Therefore, UVA has actively fostered me discovering my identity. I've learned a lot more about myself and that it makes me feel more empowered. I can be more certain about the way I feel or why things impact me the way I do. I can have a voice in certain situations. I can speak my opinion more because I am a Black woman. I have become more comfortable in my identity.

So, to me being a Black woman means I can't really give up. I have to be my own motivator. The world necessarily isn't going to help me and guide me along or give me the same opportunities that they might offer others, but that I can deal with. I try my best because I know that my best is worth something. I might not be respected as much as others in certain settings or situations, but I know I have worth and meaning. Being a Black woman, I think of all the other great strong Black women. I know that I'm not going to back down when things get hard. I have a purpose. I can do something important. I have the opportunity to help others not feel uncomfortable because of who they are. I have an expanded worldview. Sometimes it's nice to not be like everyone else and know I am different.

Chapter 11:
Kendle
1st Year

My family and I were pretty privileged.

    I went to a private middle school, and then I decided to go to a public high school to get a more diverse kind of experience. We lived in the suburbs of Greensboro, so nothing crazy, but obviously, we were pretty well off. So, coming to school and seeing how underfunded things were and how some people were struggling was kind of eye-opening. It was a public high school, so I mean, it was pretty underfunded and there wasn't anything fancy about it, but it was nice to be surrounded by people who looked like me. I was in the IB program, and then, as a freshman and sophomore, I took AP and honors. Due to the classes I was in, I was not surrounded by a majority of Black people in class. I would just see them in the hallway.

    I liked my public high school initially. Because it was different from the private middle school I went to, which was predominantly White, and I wasn't a fan of that, but eventually, I got tired of it. The school had a lot of issues. Although, going there helped me be more in touch with my race a little bit. I also was part of an organization called Jack and Jill, which is for African American youth. It's basically a family organization for mothers and children who are Black. and it basically teaches them how to be leaders and arranges family events. I became a part of it when I was four. I didn't always enjoy it. Sometimes it was kind of boring, but it helped me build community. It was a good experience overall. However, I think Jack and Jill had more of an impact than my high school because the people in Jack and Jill were more similar to me beyond just being Black. We had similar socio-economic statuses and plans to go into higher education. That helped me to form connections with people who were on the same path as me. Whereas at my school the majority of people at my school didn't have plans to go into higher education, likely because they couldn't afford it or they didn't want to. Yet, I think my high school did a decent job of preparing us for higher education, but only if you wanted that. You had to actually make an effort to learn about higher education since advising was optional. It was your own responsibility to engage with guidance counselors. I felt adequately taken care of, but that was probably just because I had the support from my parents.

    Here at UVA, in some classes, I was more surprised by the lack of Black people. Like there might be a few Asian people, then I would realize I'm the only Black person in there. So, that kind of caught me by surprise. I'm taking Intro to Data Science, Environmental Science, Plants, people, and Culture, Astronomy, and Engagements. I like the classes I have now. I feel like they're not too hard. I'm in mostly larger classes, and I'm more of a quiet person. I just do my work, and if I know somebody, I'll talk to them. I know that in some of my classes, I hardly see any other Black people, and in some classes, there are more Black people. I haven't had any negative experiences with classmates. There are some people who I'm friendly with. Some of them I talk to a little bit outside of class, but nothing excessive. I feel like the professors are pretty nice. Although, of course, they're all White. I think they're all good, at least the ones I have right now. I like most of them. Some of them aren't very good at answering questions, but they're all nice, so I can't complain. I feel supported as a student, but there's no active outward support for my identity.

I imagined that my identity would help me find community in a way by connecting with other Black people, and that has been true. I knew that UVA was predominantly White. So I knew that race might make me feel isolated sometimes if I wasn't surrounded by other Black people, which sometimes is the case. However, there are times when I still feel community because there are several Black spaces that I found. Even though it's small, I have a decent group of friends. I've gotten to know a lot of people, especially Black people from all of our circles, being intermingled and seeing them all at events. So, I've gotten to know more people than I expected. I try to go to mainly Black events. So that's been nice. There are more events specifically for Black students than I thought there would be. Events for Black students like ITCOMs, that wasn't something that I knew was gonna be an opportunity, but I'm glad that I can participate in it. It's through OAAA's Black College Women organization. ITCOMS or "In the Company of My Sisters," is a weekly discussion among a group of Black women just to talk about whatever issues we have on our minds or feel like are facing us at the moment.

There's also been a negative side of being Black here. Like events in the past few months with the hate crime at OAAA and everything, that wasn't something that I expected to happen. Although I wasn't really surprised, considering where we are geographically. Yet it was disappointing that something like that would happen here. That those kinds of people are here. I wasn't really frightened by the incident; I was just frustrated with it. Other little things have happened, like people saying slurs. I haven't experienced it firsthand, but I have heard about and sometimes witnessed other people's experiences being called slurs. It usually happens anonymously on apps like YikYak. For example, about Tichara lately, since she won student body president. There have also been situations where there's like a group of White boys, and you hear them say the "N-word." And, like, there's no Black man in that group. So obviously, one of them decided to say that word. I haven't been called it myself, but I've also heard of other people being called it on the Corner. I didn't expect those things actually to happen even though I knew it was a possibility. Now, I'm not surprised by stuff like that anymore, but it is kind of irritating, and it feels like we should be addressing the issue more and trying to educate people at least. I think that the university, in part should address it, although I don't think they plan to do that because they support free speech. Unless someone's being physically threatened, I don't think they feel obligated to do anything. But I feel like they should do something. Advocate against it or impose some kind of penalty for using slurs. They could make a system of anonymous reporting for things like that and maybe look into reaching out to those people and talking to them about it. I don't think making it more punitive is necessarily gonna help, but it shouldn't be ignored.

UVA claims to be diverse on social media and its online presence. My interpretation of diversity is centered around race or ethnicity because when you look at a person, that's what you see. I know that sometimes the intentional creation of diverse spaces is kind of frowned upon in a way here. More so by White people indirectly. For example, the backlash against Tichara and the backlash against having specific spaces for certain identities. That wasn't really what I expected. I didn't expect anybody to oppose that. Most of its online, online because people don't want to be outed. People just feel threatened by Black people gathering and making what's meant to be a Black space. They feel like they should be invited in. For example, with the multicultural center, White people might try to use it and not understand why maybe they shouldn't be there. People say UVA is self-segregated. I think that the word segregated is extreme. I think it's more just finding comfort and being around people like yourself. Especially when it's a predominantly White institution in the first place, and there are not many of us. So, I feel like gathering is a good thing and shouldn't be seen as trying to isolate ourselves from White people. Also, for example, sometimes I go to parties every once in a while. I usually go to Black parties. I like those. I don't always know all the music, but I know more people there and feel most comfortable. I've been to one White frat party. That wasn't bad. It was dirty and crowded. But I had fun. I just went once cuz one of my friends suggested it, and I enjoyed it, but not everybody enjoyed it, so we haven't gone back. At the White frat party, I didn't notice any weird looks, but I definitely heard about racist incidents happening. or suspected racist incidents, even if people didn't outwardly say anything racist.

I'm usually more comfortable being who I am when I'm surrounded by other Black people cause when you're surrounded by White people, I sometimes might feel like, oh, I don't want them to perceive me differently or negatively just because I'm Black. So I'm a little bit more reserved when in mostly White spaces. I definitely act differently depending on where I am. When you're surrounded by a certain type of people, you try to present yourself in a certain way so that you're more digestible to them. as a Black person. So I guess I kind of try to blend in a little bit more when I'm in predominantly White spaces, or at least I try not to stand out as much. I haven't been told to do that. I think it's just kind of like a subconscious thing of not wanting to make other people uncomfortable. Even though I shouldn't really care, it just feels better if I don't bring attention to myself. and the differences that I already know are there between myself and them. I guess it's not a great thing. I don't always do it intentionally; it just kind of happens. Yeah. But I wish I and everyone else could feel comfortable being the same person everywhere, regardless of who's around. But that's not always how it goes.

I'm part of EJC, which is an environmental justice collective, an environmental sciences organization, Black College Women, National Alliance on Mental Illness (NAMI), and the Virginia Dressage team. I've done horseback riding since I was like six, so it's something I've always done. Being on the team this semester has been great. However, I was on the other one last semester, and that wasn't as good, which is why I switched teams this semester. Both are predominantly White, obviously. But I feel like they were very different kinds of environments. Like the other riding team was pretty competitive, and I didn't feel supported by the other team members. I definitely felt like I was perceived and treated differently, even if they didn't realize it or do it intentionally. I also had some issues with the coach being snarky and not letting me compete. I don't know if that was based on prejudice towards me or if that was just how they treated everybody. Either way, I decided to let that go for my own sanity. I have done different types of riding. The first riding team was the type of riding that I've done for a while. But I always wanted to try the other kind of riding, So I decided to switch and try the other team. I think that's actually been better for me cause I enjoy it and it's a different group of people. It's still mainly White people - well, it's still entirely White people. Honestly, the only White people that I am friends with, I know them through horseback riding. But I think they're supportive and treat everyone fairly. They're friendlier in general than the past team. It feels less like we're competing with each other. They just seem like a more laid-back group of people.

To me, being a Black woman means being in touch with your history, which includes not-so-great things if you live in America, like civil rights and slavery and all that. It means accepting that you're gonna be the minority most of the time, but it's also a good thing because you find community in people who are like yourself. I've learned to accept my history and my position in this society and also have pride in that identity. I've always been aware of my identity as a Black woman, but that awareness has just increased over time. It probably increased a little bit more coming to UVA, whenever I'm like in a group of people or in a class I'm usually hyper aware of if I'm the only Black person. So, my identity hasn't really changed that much, but my awareness of it has increased. Sometimes, it's not a great thing to notice things like that and not be able to do anything about it. But It's also good to be conscious of where you are and how you might be similar or different from the people around you.

Chapter 12:
Mackenzie
1st Year

We grew up in military housing.

So I interacted a lot with the military kids there and we went to school together. We were very close and tight-knit, but it was hard because we were one of the few Black families living in that neighborhood so with that came its own things. Yet I always felt safe in that environment. Growing up we were middle class as was everyone else in our neighborhood. We were probably a little better off than most people because my dad was an engineer and then my mom is retired, but she was a lawyer. My high school was not really diverse. The majority of the school was White and I was one of the few Black girls there. I struggled with my hair. I would straighten it because I thought I had to straighten it to be beautiful. Once I surrounded myself with my culture and saw the braids and the locs I realized, wow, I am beautiful. I don't need to straighten my hair every day to be considered beautiful. I stopped doing that. Now I wear my natural hair out, I wear my puff and I love it. I wear braids now and I love them. That was the most defining moment because I struggled so much with my self-esteem as a Black woman, it caused me to realize the beauty of me and my culture.

Being the only Black person in a lot of situations has kind of pushed me to realize that I might be the only one in many situations, but I can still inspire other people to go into rigorous fields. I wanna go into medicine and there aren't a lot of Black doctors. I know that I have a calling over my life to become a doctor and to help people. My aunt is a physician's assistant and my mom is a lawyer. Having all these women in my life who are very strong, very educated, and supportive has really shaped me into who I am. I'm a Black woman and I'm smart. No one can tell me otherwise. I deserve to be here and be in these spaces. Even though I might be one of the only ones, I have a place here and no one can push me out of that.

My two UVA orientation leaders were both Black and that was nice. Karla and Syrell gave me the rundown of everything from day one. From orientation and just my time at the university so far I've learned more about the history of the institution and how slaves built the school and how that's reflected through the architecture like the gardens and the pavilion basements. To know that I'm going to this school and it's built by my people that was just the most shocking thing to me. I knew about it, but I didn't really know the extent of it. It's been really interesting learning the different things like how Gibbons house that was named after Isabella and William Gibbons, a couple enslaved at the school. Learning the history of that and how much Black Charlottesville played a role in the success of the school was the most surprising thing. Another surprising thing to me was how people are kind of segregated in a way still. How I've noticed it is the Black people kind of stay with the Black people and the White people kind of stay with the White people. I guess that's just being around people you feel most comfortable with. Obviously people intermingle and I do that, However, people are most comfortable with their people and that's okay too.

Coming to UVA I came prepared to be around a lot of White people, especially because of my experience in highschool. I'm glad I went through that early on because if I hadn't, I would be struggling a lot more. Now most of my friends are Black women and it's good that we can all kind of support each other and hype each other up. However, I knew it would be difficult coming here. Imma be honest, I didn't really want to come here at first because I heard what happened in 2017 and the history of the institution. I didn't really wanna come here but I knew that I could do it and that I belonged. MY dream was to always go to UCLA. My aunt and uncle went there. It is also in California and I love California. It's more diverse than here but honestly I'm really glad I came here. I'm only a first year to my second semester, so I don't have that much experience, but already I can tell, this is a school for me and it was meant to be. I feel so good here. I thought I would hate it and I thought it would be so bad and I would struggle so much. Although, I'm really enjoying it. I've met so many amazing people. My dad was a UVA fan from the very beginning. He has a cup, a UVA cup in his office and everything. My mom didn't always want me to come here, but she's been very supportive, and she thinks that this was the best school for me to go to. When I got accepted she said "This is your ancestors' wildest dreams." I didn't really think about that. I'm going to a school that was literally built by slaves, and I'm in this institution, and I'm learning from these people, and it's an amazing opportunity, and I'm truly, truly blessed to be here.

I knew college would be a different experience. There'd be certain clubs for different groups of people and there'd be so many different opportunities for different racial groups to come together. However, I still don't think UVA is diverse. It's definitely more diverse than I thought, but still not extremely diverse because I don't see larger portions of different groups of people. So I wouldn't consider UVA an extremely diverse school. When I think of a diverse institution, I think of George Mason or VCU. If I had to rate the scale of diversity here from 1 to 10, I'd say it's a five or a six. It's still extremely White.

But, and then again, we have the Latinx Center, the Multicultural Center, and the LGBTQ center. It's just nice to see spaces where people can be themselves and feel comfortable and they have all these different clubs and organizations. Seeing the performances at events like Lighting of The Lawn I was like," Wow, this is so beautiful to see in the different cultures". I enjoy experiencing people's cultures that I haven't had that chance of experiencing.

However, the lack of racial diversity here isn't always the best situation when it comes to the classroom and interacting with classmates. It's been hard trying to get people to understand my perspective of things only to be told by them "Hey, that happened in the past so it's not really affecting you now". I've had to prove myself more than other people have had to and I can already tell people think that I'm not smart and I don't belong here. Although, I do. I work hard. I try to network and reach out and put in effort so I deserve to be here. I've always been around a lot of White people most of my life, so it's never been that much of a shocker, but it still sucks to constantly have to prove yourself and show that you deserve to be here. It gets tiring and I'm kind of sick of doing that.

For example, in my chemistry study group, we had a White girl in our group and she said upfront before anything else "I wanna make sure everyone pulls their weight equally" while looking at me and my Black roommate, not the other non-Black girl. She goes on to say "I've had to do most of the work sometimes and I just wanna make sure that we're all putting in the same amount of effort cause I'm not gonna carry you guys". I was confused because me and my roommate are extremely smart people. We don't need you to carry us at all. I could just feel the aggression directed towards us because she didn't say that to the other girl. She didn't look at her for that. I clapped back and told her in response "You're not gonna need to carry me. I can do all this work on my own. And what you said wasn't very nice and respectful, so let's just work as a group, get this done and we can move on". Luckily for her, she didn't keep that behavior up, so we're good. However, that occurrence made me realize I'm gonna have to fight to prove that I am smart because people automatically think that you're gonna have to carry us. It's just the microaggressions that people have and how they try to throw digs at us. Never anything really overt, but major side eye to them. I have different responses to those microaggressions, sometimes I might try to say something and kind of pick a fight about it because I'm just so sick of hearing those things. Then at the same time, sometimes I don't wanna deal with it. So I keep quiet and won't say anything because what's the point in putting in the effort? They're not gonna care or listen to what I have to say. So my response depends on the day and if I'm feeling more empowered at the moment. I might say something back and check her but other times I don't have the energy to.

Overall my classroom experience is what I expected; a big lecture hall. What shocked me most about college, the classroom setting, and meeting people was that when you walk into a classroom, it's gonna be different each semester. You're gonna constantly meet new people and have to make new friends in those classes so you guys can work together. In high school, you didn't have to do that. I also didn't realize how much you have to network and put yourself out there, especially in those large classroom settings. I'm always thinking about medical school and how I need to reach out to my professors and talk to them about it but how am I supposed to stand with 450 people in my bio lecture? That is so hard to do. I knew I had to do that, but once you're actually in that situation, it's hard but I really make sure to raise my hand, participate and go to office hours.

Being in those Pre-med classes I can already tell it's cutthroat. People can get a little jealous of other people who raise their hand more and people will try to do anything to stand out. I can feel very anxious at times because there's just a lot going on, a lot of information being quickly thrown at you that's challenging to process. I haven't taken a calculus class so that class has been harder for me. I get anxious every time I walk into that classroom because most students know what they're doing and I don't. They're all writing the answer down and I'm still stuck on problem one. So it's definitely classroom environment is very fast paced with difficult information to process all in a cutthroat setting. Although, I like my professors. They're very helpful, very nice and very accommodating. Which I didn't anticipate because I had a mental image of them being strict (which some are), and being like "I wanna talk to you, leave me alone, I have my PhD and you're just a college student". Which is not the case at all so far.

However, I think diversity is more than just race, it also includes things like socio-economic status, gender, sexuality, and your parent's education level. Some of my friends here are more lower income, but I know people who have crazy rich parents too. Lower income wise, a lot of my friends are immigrants, so they've kind of told me their stories of how they've had to really work hard to get scholarships to help pay for college and other challenges they've had. That was very eye-opening because I didn't have to worry about paying for school because I have my dad's military stuff. I don't have to pay for all of that. One of my friends, she's from Malawi and so she could not get a laptop and so for the first couple months of school she did not have a laptop and UVA took forever to get her one. And that just I was just like come on you guys, you have billions of dollars, you can get my friend a dang laptop so she can do her architecture work. Although I haven't experienced it first hand, my friends have struggled to get money and resources from the school. To me they don't do the best job of getting it to lower income students. Majority of the students here are middle class and upper middle class so UVA probably doesn't think much about its lower income students. They don't take those students into account and they think that everyone can pay this amount of money, which is totally not the case. From what I know, I wouldn't say they don't care, but it's not on the top of their priority to provide money for those students since they have to do all this work to get what they need. It's not the easiest process.

I thought my friend group at UVA would be mostly White like it was in high school since I was the only Black girl and I'd have to struggle with that. Although, that was the exact opposite of what happens. Most of my friends here are Black. I never experienced having all of my friends be Black which has been a more amazing experience. I can be more of myself and we can make little jokes and people won't get offended. We can be ourselves and we wear our honesty around each other. We do things like taking out each other's braids. I'm so blessed to have them and being friends with them has made my UVA experience even better.

For extracurriculars, I'm in the Daniel Hale Williams Pre-Med Honor Society (DHW). It's a pre-health organization for minority students. I'm also volunteering with the Madison House. So I go to the UVA hospital once a week on Tuesday for three hours and show people around the hospital, push people in wheelchairs, and help with anything that they need in the front area of the hospital. For fun my friends and I watch movies in the lounge area. We love watching *Too Hot to Handle*. It's a messy reality show, and I love it . I'm not really much of a party person, but I'll go to a party every once in a while. I've went to Black parties. I like those. The music is good but it's definitely packed in there all the time and everyone's sweating on me. I don't wanna feel that, but it's fun to see the strolling and those parties are definitely more for me than the White parties. At one of the White frat parties my friends had an experience where they made her pay $40 to get in. She didn't pay. But, they've been charging Black students high amounts to get in, when they're technically supposed to be free. Many of my friends have had those experiences. One time when we were trying to go to White frat, we started talking to these nice White girls. I asked them "Hey, you wanna let us in?" And they let us in. However when we walked up to the party, the guys looked at us weird like they were thinking "Who are these people" or were being dismissive. Having those experiences made me realize that those kinds of parties were not for me.

When it comes to dating, that has not really happened here for me. It includes trying to figure out if they even like Black girls, which I notice is a kind of a big thing here too. Many don't. I would say this occurs across the board with all men, but especially with Black men because I've been so used to the high school I went to, they would talk down to Black about Black women. They would only like White girls and say "I would never date a Black woman. They're ghetto and loud and crazy." I didn't understand because, all right, your mom is Black, what is wrong with you? I've already kind of seen that on Grounds already. However not when it's a group of Black guys. No, they love Black women. But when it's those couple Black guys who are friends with mostly White dudes, I've definitely heard that from them.Anyways, right now I'm just not interested in dating. I'm focusing on me and working on myself.

Coming here I knew that I would have to go through things that other students probably wouldn't have to go through and face different things but I think that makes me stronger. I've always wanted to use who I am as a Black woman to inspire other people. I've always just wanted to do things that relate to the Black community and Black women. For me, I'm really interested in mental health. I know I want to focus more on that in the Black community specifically with Black women. I want to focus on how I can help them with their mental health and stuff. I always wanted to use my identity as a Black woman to just further help other Black women and be inspired by other Black women. We all hope that each generation gets better. So I hope that I wouldn't have to struggle as much and that I could help contribute to showing , I hope I could be an inspiration to Black girls if they can do whatever and be whatever they want. Because being a Black woman means being resilient despite the cards that have been dealt to us and despite all the things that we're gonna have to face. We're so strong and we can accomplish truly anything. Therefore, I'm going to continue being resilient and strong. However, I don't wanna be that all the time because I'm allowed to cry and be emotional in addition to being a strong, independent, and selfless person.

My understanding of being a Black woman has changed since coming to UVA because I've seen more diversity in different areas of study. For example, a lot of my friends are in engineering school and that is crazy hard. So, seeing different people that look like me going into these really cool fields, it's definitely a game changer because back in high school and stuff I thought I couldn't do that because I'm Black and it wasn't for me. Being here and seeing all of these Black women go into different fields that are just so cool, so amazing has taught me " Hey, you can do this and that there are so many things in place that are gonna help you get there, and people in your life that, wanna see you succeed and do well and that relate to your experiences." So, I realized how supported I am since coming here and that I can do this. I'm more empowered now.

I'm very excited for the future and I feel very empowered. I have goals that I need to reach and I'm willing to put in that work and effort to get there. I'm willing to be uncomfortable in certain situations and to really put myself out there. Although I consider myself to be more introverted until I feel comfortable around people I'm working on breaking outta that shell and putting myself out there. I'm really excited for the future. I know I have time and there are just so many cool opportunities and things to do here. I'm looking forward to just continuing to meet so many cool people, continuing my journey of going to medical school, experiencing more of my culture, and my people and maybe getting into dating. I want to continue building and strengthening the relationships that I have here and getting closer to my friends.

Chapter 13:
L.P

I was born and raised in Philadelphia.

I live in West Philly. I'm from a predominantly urban middle- and lower-class neighborhood, about 95% of my neighbors are African American. Drexel University is two blocks from where I live. The University of Pennsylvania is like six blocks the other way. It's a neighborhood that is now becoming gentrified because the universities are literally taking over. It's not what it was when I was growing up.

There are a lot of four-story homes now, a lot of apartment complexes, less parking garages, less trees. They're building a track center. It's kind of good at the same time because now we have a new park and new kinds of restaurants. We didn't have a Walmart or a Target. Gentrification was also good in that respect because before it was a food scarce area. We didn't have a major supermarket. You needed to drive to get to a supermarket. But now we got supermarkets, like Whole Foods and Acme. Bringing in those types of businesses which are heavy on organic and fresh foods, was a plus.

But it was also a negative because a lot of people I grew up with were forced to move out of my neighborhood. I'm seeing people lose their homes. Now my dad and my mom are running into the issue where every year someone comes and asks to buy our home: "Can we buy your home? We'll pay for this amount. Can we buy your home?" Then seeing my childhood neighbor friend's parents choose to sell their home when financial issues happened, hit close to home. It's kind of scary being so close to gentrification. We're straddling the borderline. Like we own our home, we own cars, but still face economic issues.

I went to a Magnet high school, Central High School, that was in a nice part of Philly. Prior to coming to UVA, I had already attended schools that were predominantly Asian or people from a White ethnic background. I was surrounded by people that were demographically and racially different than me. It was like UVA in that aspect. I was often the only Black woman in some of my classes, particularly like the International Baccalaureate classes. There probably would be me and one other non-White person, who might not have been a woman necessarily and even Black. It might be just me and one other minority student. Someone that's Latinx or perhaps Indian. In that respect, it's like the University of Virginia (UVA). I was already adjusted to an environment that lacked people who looked like me and related to me.

When you first start high school, it's kind of a scary experience, but then you start to find your circle of people. People who value you, who connect with you. They look past race or class differences. When you find those group of people, it becomes easier. School doesn't become such a hassle. And Philadelphia is an urban city that has a lot of things that cater to the younger generation. Our downtown area is huge. It has a bunch of shopping centers, a lot of restaurants. It's just like a good environment to grow up in. So, after school, you have plenty of opportunities to hang out with your friends and do activities, if that makes sense.

One reason I liked my high school was because it was surrounded by a bunch of other high schools that were predominantly Black. And like I said, the after school atmosphere was a bunch of crazy stuff. It probably wasn't something I should like since it was just a bunch of young kids being downtown doing random things. I liked that experience, that chaotic atmosphere, of the after school experience. It made me like my high school. If that makes sense. I just really like the after school environment because even if you attended the same school, you didn't know each other. After school, you can end up having a conversation with a complete stranger, but now you have friends that go to another school that's nearby. Now you guys are linking up at the Wendy's. That's what I really liked because my school people were like UVA people who are like stay to themselves. They focus on academics. They were like kind of quiet and shy. I like talking, I like people who are like outgoing. It made it easier to literally meet a bunch of random friends.

I do feel I have social economic advantages since I was able to go to magnet schools compared to other people who may be my race or gender. However, within these schools, I did feel like I was subjected to racism and biases and stereotypes. In my high school. During like the whole Black Lives Matter movement, we had a list of demands. The movement really pushed us to advocate for changes. One of them was getting an equity advisor, changing the penal system. We realized drugs became an issue at my school, but only specific people were getting expelled. Others were only receiving detention or in school suspension. We felt like advanced courses were not being pushed enough to minority students. I did see some changes. And I still speak to people from my high school. We are continuing that battle. Within my institution, I felt like there were a lot of needs of change the same way. I feel like that for UVA still has a lot of prejudices. Things that happened here still need areas of improvement. However, on the overall scheme, I'm still able to come here and attend.

Honestly, I did not do any research on UVA before applying. At school, we had like counselors that assisted you and gave you a list of the top institutions. This is how UVA became on my list of "apply to" universities. But even in applying, I wasn't really enthusiastic to come here. I actually knew nothing about this school. I just applied and then I happened to get the most financial aid from UVA. Then like I did a virtual tour. The virtual tour made me nervous because I come from a big city. I'm not seeing anything at UVA and Charlottesville. And when I got here, I realized like the Charlottesville area doesn't cater to a college demographic. It's so odd to go to a school that's in a small city that is basically built around UVA but doesn't even cater to UVA students. That made me worry even before coming here. And when I got to UVA, I realized this is really not a fit for me. But because of the financial aid package, I decided to tough it out and that maybe I need some change; maybe the lack of the lack of activity here would be able to keep me focused. The lack of activity has helped me focus, but it's also been depressing. It's extremely depressing because there's such a small Black community here.

You can't stereotype Black people; everyone's different. They come from different upbringings. But, in my experience, most of the demographic here come from wealth. I don't relate with some Black people within my own community. This is even more depressing because it's already a small pool of us, but that pool even shrinks amongst class distinction. I just often be getting depressed because I feel like I can't fit in with certain people. I'm finding areas where I there are people that I feel I can talk to, but it does kind of feel depressing I feel like UVA don't even contribute within the community. They're building a hotel, but we need a Black cultural center for Black people. We share a cultural center with all the other races, yet there's also a Language Commons or a Latinx center directly for some student populations. Why can't we have our own cultural center?

I also feel like they're constantly buying up apartments, constantly, expanding the university. Yet Charlottesville's downtown area is so undeveloped. Basically, most people's income in Charlottesville is based on UVA. People who are natives here, they work for the university. Everything is centered around UVA. It's such a trillion-dollar industry. You would think UVA would help to expand the downtown area, build more activities. I feel like they can do so much more. I feel like the lack of activities only heightens the stresses people feel. People feel like they have to drop out because there is no other outlet. If you don't join the club or if you don't make friends, you're just here living afloat. And that's completely hard because where do you go? You don't always want to go to the library or go on Grounds. to get away. There should be another space far from the school. Personally, I feel like UVA needs to work on this issue.

I feel coming here, I already knew who I was. I have like pretty good confidence. I don't know, maybe it's, because I'm from Philly. I'm from like a predominantly Black city, so I'm super comfortable in myself. Coming here I know I'm a dark-skinned African American woman. I'm heterosexual. I already know who I was as a person. I felt safe. I really didn't feel like I need to adjust or that I needed to even pay attention those type of categories. I already was content. I'm trying to say that it wasn't much of a thought process before arriving here. But as soon as I got here, I had a transition class that was basically minority students and that was taught by a Black professor. She basically explained what happened during the Unite the Right rally prior to us getting to UVA. She told us about someone getting ran over by a KKK member during the event. It bothered me that I didn't know about this event. I should have done research. I didn't even know that UVA was built by enslaved laborers until like my Spring Semester when I finally went on the tour. Oh my god, I felt so horrible not knowing these things. I don't even go to the Lawn anymore. I just walk through, go to the corner, then walk back. I don't really like going to the lawn. That was crazy to hear about.

I felt like being a Black student, I should know this history. I was letting my ancestors down. Coming here with high hopes and not even knowing the history is crazy. It definitely would have like been in the back of my head. It probably would have caused me to reconsider my decision of coming here. That bothered me for a while. Then I began to see comments written on walls, a noose put around a statue at UVA, and students referring to other students with racial slurs. We're supposed to be moving forward and moving above this racial tension. Yet, I'm coming into an institution that is predominantly White and the administrators are not saying anything. It was mind boggling to me that they would release statements after the noose incident saying the issue was investigated, but I never saw the results of the investigation. It was really a shock coming here.

I actually thought there would be more Black people at UVA. We were coming here during the Covid years. I was really desperate to get out the house. I missed my junior and senior year of high school. I just want to go to college. I'm just ready to get up and go. I was just like hoping that a college of 60,000 students would have Black people. There has to be Black people. Then get here and I'm like, damn. . . It's like 500 of us. Where everybody at? That was my experience. I thought it would be a White majority, but I didn't think it would be so small a Black community here with 60,000 students. That was crazy. You can have a class and you might be the only Black person. I'm in a discussion class and I'm literally the only minority. It's like, "God damn."

I'm looking for social diversity in my classes. I want to explore how your race impacts your life and society. I am looking to be with students that can relate, to some extent, on how race can lead to disadvantages in society, even if it is in economic terms. I'm deeply passionate about issues such as crime, race, and power. I take a lot of classes that are philosophically or sociologically focused within African American Studies. In my sociology class, there are students from a diversity of European heritages, but they are not going to have the same experiences as me socially. And sometimes I find my classes don't take into consideration how what they are saying about race might be offensive.

For example, in my philosophy class last year, we were talking about how people obtain legal rights. My TA was talking about how Black people were not considered to be legal persons. Therefore, they weren't required to have legal rights. Usually in my philosophy classes, we then note that's how it was historically but this is not the case today. But my TA used the example of women to make this point, but noted Black people are still facing issues. And we wondered, "Well, what are you really trying to say? Do you think we are legal persons or not?" There were only four of us in class. She made eye contact with us and it just really seemed like she was saying that we still aren't deserving of legal rights.

The way she delivered it to her class was really racist, like it was really racist. She didn't even try to smooth it out. And you could see the difference with how she explained the issue when discussing women. You could see how with people with mental disabilities that even today they still aren't considered as having legal rights because they lacked "the capacity" to legally speak up for themselves. I was like why don't you approach the issue about Black people, with the same level of sensitivity?" Discuss how with the mass enslavement of Black people and, even after Jim Crow, Black People were not considered people. She did say we were considered "property," but she made it seem we lacked a mental rationale to speak up for ourselves because of these experiences. Like we were mentally inferior.

It was strange because even the White people in our class were looking like, "Bro…." Everyone's face was confused. She was like, Black people lack rationality. They're not capable people. They are aggressive. She went into the whole aggressive stereotype. I was really angry. After class, I emailed my TA and my professor. He gave us an apology in class. I don't know what he did behind doors, but she sent us a short apology email before class. But I still don't think like she truly understands the importance of understanding these social contexts. She doesn't understand that you cannot teach these types of issues without addressing those contexts first. People like to leave race and historical context out of the discussion. But race is so important.

I have agency at such moments. I am going to say something regardless. But I'm also saying, I'm taking a risk doing so. I'm taking a risk by speaking up because I don't know what the consequences are going to be. There could even be like retribution. Like maybe they'll try to come back at me. I have had instances where teachers will say, "Well maybe you're seeing it the wrong way. Maybe you're looking at it too politically." And I'm like, "No, I'm not." So, I'm always going to say something because if I don't, who's going to say something? Someone else might be feeling the same way. Hopefully, they will hear me. This was actually the most at this school that I heard. That a professor did something, that the professor got into addressing the issue.

I don't know what I thought about the meaning of being a Black woman at UVA or being a Black woman, in general, before coming here. I hate being asked that question. But I like my darker skin more after coming here. I'm in all these clubs I model for Fashion For a Cause (FFC). I model for Runway. I model for Africa Day. They take a bunch of photos. Having all these photos taken, having people like constantly say, "Oh, your skin! Do you want to model?" It really made me like my skin more than prior to being here. I'm not going to lie. I was happy being dark-skinned, but I also had like issues internally with my skin, with the complexion. Coming here made me love myself more, specifically in consideration at my skin. So, coming to UVA, seeing how a lot of the Black women love themselves, love their skin, really embracing of it? That's something I really love about UVA and I'm thankful for it.

But in the larger context, being a Black woman means being ignored, being condemned to being considered aggressive. It means living with the fear of confirming stereotypes. I also know that being with a Black woman just comes with constantly being under surveillance, constantly being judged, constantly being put into a box. It can feel like you're walking on eggshells But I'm just not going to be put in that box. I really don't care how anyone views me. It's me. That's just part of my personality. I am lucky to have this type of personality. I literally just reached the conclusion that I really don't care. I'm going to be myself. Some people are going to like it. Other people are not going to like it.

Chapter 14:
Arianny
4th Year

Being born in the Dominican Republic is really an interesting space when considering the diaspora and how Blackness manifests on the island.

In the Dominican Republic, I would be considered a darker complexion, at least in the neighborhood that I was in. Growing up, being considered dark, my mom and dad always taught me just how to navigate the world better so that my skin color didn't become a means that people could utilize to weaponize my existence.

That became completely different when I came to the United States. Before university I lived in Boston my entire time in the U.S. It's no secret that Boston is a pretty predominantly White city, as many cities in America are. Although my neighborhood, in particular, was what they would call a melting pot, there were instances when I was positioned to question if my experiences were valid or if my insights would have any merit behind them just because of my simple existence and that I'm different from those around me.

I jokingly say this, but coming to America definitely made me lose some melanin. But then again, I was literally on an island where like the sun was beaming and it was 90 degrees every day. Growing up in the Dominican Republic, I would always be called a term of endearment, or at least as it came across, Negra, which means Black. So, from a very early age, I ingrained it into my identity. Now, for example, when I came to see how it impacted my childhood, I noticed that my grandmother on my mother's side who has some Spaniard ancestry in her, and she's very much so fair-skinned blue eyes, would treat me differently than my cousins who have a lighter complexion. She says that it wasn't a difference, and I just overthink situations. But I definitely noticed a difference from how I was treated. That difference in treatment also manifested in the school setting that I was a part of. I went to a Catholic private school in the Dominican Republic. A lot of the time, I was often the darkest one in the class. That definitely impacted my childhood looking back, but back then, I would joke like, "Oh, boys don't like me because of my skin color". Now I know that definitely wasn't a joke. It was very real despite me being super young. I think that the erasure of Blackness on the island is something that becomes ingrained in somebody as soon as they're born due to who we've had formerly lead the country, and then his racist ideologies just transcend over generations and generations.

It wasn't until I got to community college, because I did go to community college before UVA, that I heard the word Afro-Latina. Even in high school, I wasn't hearing words like Afro-Latina or certain terminology that people are now coining to take ownership and agency over their identity, which I'm all for. But to me, I never saw myself as a mix of two things. For example, Afro-Latina was something that I first heard back in

2021. While growing up, watching the Del, which is a Spanish soap opera, I would never classify or consider myself to be Latina because I didn't see myself in the media.I was like, okay, like I know that I'm Dominican and I'm Black. It just, that's how it manifests. How that impacted my college experience, I don't know if I had any expectations at all. I can certainly say that while I didn't have any expectations, I was welcomed into UVA's Black community, and I was never questioned about where I'm from or questioned about my experiences and my identity. As a Black woman, for the first time ever, it just made me feel as if I belonged somewhere without having to force my way in. That was something really nice I experienced, especially coming from Boston, where I've never seen so many Black students in one place be together at the same time. So, coming to UVA was rather a welcoming and nice experience.

In high school, my experience was one where I felt that I had to box myself in to fit with White students for the simple fact that I was only in honors and AP classes. Oftentimes, I would be one of about five out of a group of 30 students that were POC. So it was a really interesting space because I was aware that I wasn't like these people, but I had to mold myself through the clothes that I wore, how I styled my hair or the verbiage that I used to make sure that I'm not adhering to certain tropes that these people have developed of what I'm supposed to be in their head. Which, of course, any normal fifteen-, sixteen-, or seventenn-year-old high school girl is dealing with when unearthing certain parts of her personality. Therefore, that experience for me was no different than the average high schooler, whether that be Black, Hispanic, or whatever the case may be. Although, to me, my experience was unique in the sense because of the spaces that I was in, I had to behave in certain ways that not only limited what I wanted to do or be who I am by further boxing me in. However, when I got to community college, that was a breath of fresh air. Community College was different in the sense that it was the true definition of a melting pot. Yet, there were still certain parts of my identity in high school that I attached to.

It wasn't until I started traveling outside of Boston and meeting more Black people that I felt comfortable in certain settings and spaces where I could finally take a breath of fresh air and be like, okay, I don't have to live in this real fake reality anymore. I can just be myself. To this day, I'm very much cognizant of how that could sometimes slip up in my behavior, even at UVA. UVA is an interesting place because a lot of the times you're questioned if you really belong or certain merits and traumas are assigned to you because you're here. For example, it's again no secret that the university is majority White students, being oftentimes the only Black person in a classroom, everybody's probably looking at me. They are subconsciously probably thinking this girl's different than us, where does she come from? These biases, whether it's intentional or not, it's not for me to say. Yet I'm sure that that just comes with the White experience. I feel their energy, I know that it makes certain people uncomfortable. I'm always in a position where I not only have to overcompensate, but I'm always having to do more than my White counterparts or just feel the need to prove that I'm good enough to be here when there are people that are just here. I don't have the privilege just to be, I always have to be on my tippy toes just in case I slip up; I'm not adhering back to those certain tropes like, there goes the Black girl acting out. It's been a vicious cyclical cycle from high school to UVA, having to mold and confine as to what's too Black. What's not too Black? Is she being ghetto? Is she being bossy? It's really just never-ending.

I'm actually grateful that I experienced what I experienced so early on because now I am super confident in myself. I don't shy away from speaking on anything that I don't see as appropriate behavior or if I ever feel like I'm being gas-lit by my White classmates, which happens pretty often. I'm very quick to call that out. I also will say that just like the same way that I had those experiences in community college, I also did work in corporate America for four years. I started working in corporate at a very early age, from 19 all the way up until I was 22. These racist practices and notions were already embedded into my head, like, this is what the real world is like. Although those experiences have given me the power to realize if something isn't to my liking or if I feel a certain way about it, I'm definitely going to speak up. I think that anybody can vouch that I'm very outspoken. I'm not gonna take anything that I don't see as acceptable. I won't let it fly, but it all ties back to my experiences from being a young high school girl.

I did not know about UVA until 48 hours before the application was due. I actually called one of my best friends, and I told her, "Hey, I am having a really hard time. I need to transfer schools." My ideal school at the time was the University of Pennsylvania. Even then, when curating my transfer school lists, I never thought about diversity or anything because I wanted to be accepted and fit into what the "American dream" would consider the epitome of success. Therefore, I overlooked certain things, such as diversity or clubs. I was asking does this program fit my needs.

After I found out about UVA, I was like, "Okay, this is cool". I noticed I was able to come in as a Batten School transfer and thought it was perfect and fit everything that I wanted. I then convinced myself that I could get in and UVA would be like my safety school should everything else fail. And I kind of just let it go and never really looked back. Then it didn't really register with me until like a month and a half later after I sent that application out when I realized, wait, the University of Virginia was where the Unite the Right rally happened back in 2017 when I graduated high school. Which was something I should have looked more into. To me, Virginia is not the South. However, looking at what the media was portraying, I was like, okay, this is the South. So maybe they have certain races, ideologies and practices embedded into their way of life, which then made me wonder about who's gonna be my community. How is this going to work? What's gonna happen? I then took it upon myself to research and find clubs on grounds outside of the Virginia Consulting Club, which I wrote about in my personal statement because I came from a consulting background. Then I found BSA, and I found that they were looking to fill the CFO position, and I was like, "Oh my God, this is perfect. I'll apply." I secured that alongside my position as President of Black Student Leaders and Policy. I came to UVA with the mission to enter the space and just be as involved as I can within the Black community. However, After reading some statistics, I realized there are not even 13% of Black students at UVA, only four to 6%. I thought, "Oh my God, this is bad". But when I got to UVA, I realized this was my 6%. I laser-focused on my community, making it so specific to people who look like me and come from the same backgrounds or as adjacently as possible to my background so I only focused on what was going on in the Black community. I don't really know what White students are up to. And to be honest, I don't really have the interest to know what's going on, outside of like what I see on CAV daily or the sports. But that's my long-winded way of saying that I went from being, I don't wanna say ignorant, but unknowing what diversity and inclusion and just community looked like and could have manifested in at UVA to being very laser focused within the Black community.

I really resonate with the level of togetherness within the Black community at UVA because growing up Dominican means having the essence of community entrenched into your daily life. For example, in my neighborhood, I knew that while I lived in a predominantly White city, I could go to certain pockets of Boston, and there would be Dominican salons where we would all commune together, even within my family. So, I was really taught what an effective and reliable community looked like from an early age. And I can definitely say that the ideals that I was brought upon, like respect, being there unconditionally for one another, and being of service to your community, definitely were present at UVA. I've had instances that I thought were going to end my time here at the university, not only as a student but also brought me down to this dark mental rabbit hole. However, what really pulled me through was my community here. UVA has resources like CAPS, and you can talk to your professors, but at the end of the day, those resources weren't the change makers in my reality and what allowed me to be where I am today, with a healthy mental state. It wasn't those resources; it was my community that made that change possible. Knowing that I could count on friends who would do whatever they could make possible to ensure that I was either getting a certain set of notes or connecting with my classmates to tell me who to reach out to when escalating a problem. That's what's really made the difference and not these resources that White UVA promotes.

I came to UVA as a Batten student, and to be honest, I did not know how elite the Batten School was until I got to UVA. When I applied, it seemed like the perfect fit for me because Professor William was doing a lot of work with police brutality, which I did research on back home. So, I thought that the Batten School would be the perfect program for me. I came in as a direct transfer student from community college to Batten. Little did I know, I was in many ways screwed over by admin because I was supposed to take two classes before I arrived on grounds to fulfill being a full Batten student, which they didn't tell me. That then became a problem because I had professors, who at the time weren't accommodating to the life situations that I had going on. For example, one of my friends got sentenced to life in prison. My grandmother got really sick and I was moving from Boston to Virginia by myself. It was the first time that I'd ever left my home. So there was a lot going on. I unfortunately had professors that didn't really budge or care. Instead, they were like, "Hey, sorry, um, Batten has a certain requirement you have to meet" and there's a 3.4 GPA requirement, which drove me to the brink. I'm like, "I can't do this., I am not about to compete at the undergraduate level with people over a major. I'm just not doing it." So I dropped out of the major. A lot of people were like, "Oh, why would you do that? Like, Batton is so elite". And I'm like, "Look, I just don't have the mental stamina to be dealing with administrative issues or whatever the case may be."

Now, when I got to the history department, as a history major, literally all of my administrative troubles were alleviated. Also, I no longer had to compete with other students to prove my self-worth. I could just explore my interests and do what I like to do. However, on the cultural side, similar to Batten, nothing really changed as I'm often the only Black student in class. And a lot of the time, as I mentioned earlier, it just positions your White classmates to give you that look. Which is an interesting occurrence, because I take a lot of classes centered around slavery. Which is also very different from Batten courses because there I was taught how to become a good leader through civic leadership, team dynamics, and public policy.

So Batten represents the corporate-government route. Now, this side is kind of like the arts and exploring humanities, where it's not really a numbers game, it's more so concerning historical accounts, and how those occurrences have impacted America. Being in spaces with White students where I'm like, reliving trauma that I didn't even experience, but my ancestors did, by their ancestors, is super uncomfortable because I know these conversations need to be had, but I don't wanna be the token Black student voicing the plight of the entire Black community. I don't know what that is remotely like to the extent other populations of Black people have experienced.

I'm also part of the History Distinguished Majors (DMP) honors program, and I'm one of the only two Black students. Even in that space, I feel like I don't belong. I feel like my ideas have a lot of value, but when I look around at my classmates and see what their research ideas are, it makes me realize this gap that prevails between Black and White America. For example, I have White classmates who are researching abortion, animal rights, pubs, White widows in the Confederacy, or the history of railroads. And here I am looking at how the FDR New Deal exacerbated living inequalities amongst Black Americans and how that still prevails in the 21st century. And it's like, okay, wow, two completely different realities. I'm sure that their research has value and merit, but my experience doesn't position me to think about something quirky like researching animal rights. I'm more focused on what my community and my people have experienced.

If I were to go through my university selection all over again, I one hundred percent, without a doubt, would choose to go to a PWI. Being at a PWI definitely has value. My experience as a formerly undocumented immigrant from the Dominican Republic and all the adversity that I've faced while being at a university like UVA has led me to ignore when people say, "Oh, you got in because of X, Y, Z, blah, blah, blah." I know that I am here because I belong, whether the university wants to use me as a metric for diversity or whatever that's on them. I'm in spaces where once people who look like me weren't even allowed to be in. So being here is definitely more powerful than being at an HBCU because being at a HBCU is very tied to the African American experience, and I'm sure that African students or a number of Black students go to HBCUs, but to me, that would not have been as impactful as being at a PWI. I take ownership and agency over the fact that I am different. I'm not supposed to be here yet; I'm here, and I'm making strides. Also, I recognize the notoriety that UVA brings. When I would tell people, oh yeah, I go to community college, I would always get a dismissive, oh, okay. People would think I go to community college because I'm dumb or I didn't get certain grades in high school. Little do people know I was forced to go to community college because I couldn't afford university due to my legal status. I never qualified for financial aid and didn't wanna put my parents through debt. Now, the tone that people adopt when I say I go to the University of Virginia is different. Oftentimes people tell me, "Oh, that's the baby ivy." It's very interesting how people perceive you based on the branding of your school. So, I will always take pride in going to a PWI.

At UVA, I'm not as involved in the Latinx community as I could be because I feel that there's definitely more tension and a sense of dominance amongst the Latinx community here. I can say that, being from the Dominican Republic, my country is viewed as lesser than a country like Mexico. I think mindset subconsciously manifests here on grounds in certain ways, whether people would like to admit it or not. Even just the way that Dominicans speak, we're always said to speak the "ghetto Spanish." There's been times when I've heard that to be like a running joke here. Whenever I go to the Latinx student center, I'm like, this is why I don't really associate with the Latinx community here. Although, I do have good Latino friends. But this is as far as it'll go within the Latinx community versus the Black community where I'm on, like 10 executive boards and going to events and just hanging out with Black students. So, I have a very different experience between the two communities.Like any community, there are times when there are differences in how we do things or cattiness from students. I will say that the amount of support and energy I've received from the Black community here at UVA is unmatched. There have been, unfortunately, times of intense divide within the community, but at the end of the day, I think that we're all bound by the fact that not only are we Black students in a space that was literally not designed for us, but we're also coming together because we see and understand each other's plights, which makes it that much closer despite whatever calamities and disputes come before us.

However, my dating experience here has just been a joke. Like to simply put it into one word, it's been a joke. I actually came across a TikTok where it was like, oh, UVA is where you're meant to find the love of your, of your life. I'm like, not if you're Black. If you're Black, relationships here aren't a thing. Within Black UVA, from what I've noticed, has definitely not been a thing. Like hookup culture is more prominent than relationships. There might be a couple of people who are seen together, and people we know who go together, but nothing's ever been official. And that is also my experience as well because I, I'll talk or get to know one or two people a semester, but it's just for fun because it's temporary. Since it's just temporary, and it really doesn't have value. I'm sure that probably looks different on an HBCU campus. Therefore, I think my dating experience definitely applies to Black women in general here. White women at UVA have it differently. The amount of my White classmates who are in relationships is wild. It's, I'm like, "Oh my God. How did you find somebody here?" Even Asian women have an easier time dating here. But with Black women, it's just not good for us here. It's real bad, the dating pool is very much contaminated.

As a Dominican woman, I was raised not on the idea but on the reality that I've always been Black. Living in the Dominican Republic, I had a reality of what it meant to be Black. Now, being in America, that's a different reality because my Blackness is always questioned. It's either I'm not Black enough, or it's just a lot of moving parts. But in the essence of what it means to be a Black woman, I can speak from my experience as a light-skinned Black woman. I know that I have certain privileges that dark-skinned Black women don't have. But to be a Black woman in America definitely means always to have had your experiences invalidated. Moreover, just living in the shadows and almost viewed as second-class citizens.

Being at UVA made me realize that being Black is not a monolith. That's the biggest thing that UVA highlighted for me was the differences within the diaspora. I'm not African American, I don't adhere to and have never practiced certain African-American cultural practices, like going to church, for example, and using certain cultural verbiage. However, that also makes me realize that just because I'm not African-American doesn't mean that I'm not Black. It's made me even more comfortable with taking pride in my Caribbean roots because, to me, there's still a stark difference between Caribbean culture and Latin American culture. I will never in my life relate to what Mexicans experience or what the media projects of White Mexicans, which is part of Latin American experiences in Argentina or Colombia, which is a country still heavily populated with Black people. But for me, just knowing that there's that disdain towards my culture and the Caribbean UVA has not only highlighted that through the courses that I've taken but it's made me take pride in saying that I'm Afro-Caribbean. That's typically the term that I go by. Of course, I always just say I'm Black. But when people ask, "Oh, what's your group?", I say Afro-Caribbean because I don't want to dishonor my Black roots, considering both my parents are Black. Yet, I'm also from the Caribbean. So, being at UVA made me realize that those two things can coexist, but also, at the same time, I don't have to adhere to this monolith of Blackness.

Chapter 15:
C.R

I'm from a suburb of Prince William County.

I don't know how to describe it really, but it's a suburb. I lived in the part that was on the borderline of being upper-middle-class. In my early years, I went to a private school, but that private school was predominantly Black and diverse. It was nice growing up in that environment. I remember in third grade, I transferred to a public school, which I didn't mind, but it was definitely a rough transition with the learning styles, of course. Then I went to a Middle School, which is also, that was predominantly Black and Latino and mixed socioeconomically. Being in those environments shaped me in a way, so when I did go to my high school, which was predominantly White, I did have this backbone. It was definitely an adjustment, but I would say I did have this reassurance of knowing who I was as a Black person, and I could go to this White environment, and I won't be, you know, changed. I won't be necessarily influenced by what they do or how they present themselves.

My family has played a big role in how I view myself as a Black woman. Especially having a mother who's also the head of the household. Obviously, a lot of Black moms take on that role. My parents are married, however, her decision is final. She definitely has a huge impact on who I am as a Black woman and what to expect and how much work we have to put in. You know, we have to do twice the amount of work, of course, you know, White people, but also twice the amount of work of also Black men and that, the pressure that comes with that and so much is expected of us.

At first, I was anxious after deciding to come to UVA because Charlottesville is kind of diverse area but UVA is not as diverse of an institution in comparison. You can't really escape UVA. When you walk off campus, you're still in Charlottesville where UVA still has a big presence. UVA takes up such a large portion of the city space physically and invisibly. My friends applied to schools that were in DC. I have a friend that goes to GW and one who goes to Georgetown and, they like it because those schools are in a metropolitan city so they have experiences with other people from different cultures and backgrounds. But here there's not much to do or see.

I remember when I came for orientation, I felt that solidified my prejudgments based upon my experience of being a Black woman at UVA. My leaders were amazing, I had Lauren and Sergio. I remember we were grouping for the first time and after the e in-troduction we went outside and I said, hi to this one White girl she didn't acknowledge me. Sergio noticed that and he talked to me about it later, which I liked. However, that incident just set a sour mood for the whole orientation. I told my parents about how I was upset because I tried to talk to them, but a lot of 'em came off rude. They didn't acknowledge me, were not respectful and it was very unpleasant the whole time. However, I was thankful for my orientation leaders Lauren and Sergio. I talked to them the whole time and befriended them cause the rest of my group was very cliquey. They were even disrespectful towards my orientation leaders.

I feel like when I finally got to UVA during welcome week, I actually did like being here because I got to see more Black people. I went to a cookout that day. I got to see and be surrounded by other Black people. That was definitely helpful to me and comforting. I did see some of my friends from high school that came here and that was definitely comforting as well. Especially a particular friend. She's a Black woman and being around her has definitely comforted me here. We comfort each other. She has a Black roommate and we have a friend group. So it's nice. That first week in that first month was good. However, after the hate crime at OAAA and the noose, that was when I found out, wow, y'all really don't like us here. But it was definitely comforting seeing how the Black community here sticks together even though it is small. I was definitely surprised by how close-knit everyone was.

When I first got here, I noticed every time I went to any dining location on Grounds, all the workers were Black. I remember this one key experience at one of the meal exchange places I always go to. At The Castle, all of their staff is Black except for an older White guy. At The Castle, I always say thank you when I get my food and try to talk to the workers. Yet, I noticed that no one else said thank you or talked to them. I'm so confused by that. These are the people serving us. There are people with feelings too, and they're cooking your food. They are nourishing you. They're people, they're human too. I also tried to investigate why there are so many Black workers within that industry. I remember talking to one of my professors who's one of the professors in the COLA class that I'm taking. He said UVA has a contract with this one company called Aramark. Aramark hires out these Black workers on a contract basis and they control their wages which are very low. I was just talking with him about it, and I wasn't that surprised. I would say our school president has been good, but I would say UVA itself comes off as progressive and liberal when they're not. They're playing into and feeding into these systems that they're publicly denying their part in. If you play into them, why are you condemning at the same time? I just find that annoying since I've been here.

I think UVA has people from different socioeconomic backgrounds, ethnicities, and races of course. But I don't think that they promote diversity the way they say they do. The amount of Black and Latino students that there are here is so low. Many students, especially the White ones often come from wealthy backgrounds. I've noticed when I talk to people, usually other White students, either one of their siblings or one of their parents went here and none of my parents went here. No one in my family went here. So, I would say I had some animosity towards being here at UVA. Cause my ancestors were here, and that's just weird. I'm basically reaping the benefits of what they built. And I feel weird even coming here because they were enslaved here. Also on my maternal grandmother's side, they were enslaved workers here. So, I've had some animosity towards that. I don't know how to take that. I'm reminded every time I cross the lawn that Thomas Jefferson basically did own my ancestors, and even being reminded every day of the history of the university. Every time I walk around and look at the grounds, the question is not do I deserve to be here, but should I be here? I had a friend ask me, why would you go to a school that your ancestors were literally enslaved on? I don't know how to answer that. I genuinely don't know how to answer that. I do feel guilty, but at the same time, I could create my own legacy in a different way than they did because they were forced to be here.

Anyway, I don't think UVA provides everything racially and culturally diverse students need. Although they do provide safe spaces for them, I don't like just giving a community a room like I know they did, Latinx Center or the Multicultural Center. I feel like those safest spaces, specifically the MSC have been taken up by White students. I mean White students you could clearly tell they're White Americans. What cultural background do they come from? Why are they taking up these spaces that are not necessarily meant for them? I feel they should be mindful of the space that they're in.

UVA needs to step up to provide the actual necessities for Black students of different backgrounds. I feel they don't provide but I would say the Office of African American Affairs is a good space and source for Black students. However, I also wish it was a place for all Black students, no matter who you are, African-American or not. I don't think the organization should be renamed, but they should be more explicit that OAAA is for all Black American students. I have some friends who are African, their parents they're first generation or second generation and they don't know that they could use the same resources that the OAAA provides beyond just going to events.

Generally speaking and at UVA, there's a huge difference in the way that Black women are seen. We're masculated and there are all these stereotypes against us that honestly harm us. For example, colorism. Not that I have to deal with it, but I know my other Black girlfriends have to deal with that as well. And issues with texturism and having to present yourself a certain way where you won't be perceived as ghetto, promiscuous, or just masculine, and it's just annoying, and I've experienced that growing up.

Either way, identifying as a Black woman, I take 100% pride in it. We're the blueprint for pretty much everything. We basically carry this whole Black community on the backs of us, and constantly, we're being told that we're not good enough or stereotypes being placed on us. After all this adversity, we're still here. We're still that group. We're still that person. You know, I would say, Black women, even though they're the most disrespected person on the planet, we are the most - I don't wanna say strong cause I hate repeating the "strong Black woman" stereotype. But I would definitely say we're the most persistent people. However, I hate it when people try to place that stereotype on us and want us to take on all of our community struggles. A lot of Black men don't wanna take on responsibility even though even in the civil rights movement, Black women were carrying us, and even with Black Lives Matter, we're still carrying that movement. I don't like the pressure that's placed on us to be this type of strong person. I wish we could be vulnerable at times and not let our vulnerability be taken as anger or something negative. I'm sick and tired of that.

Endnotes

1. Miller, Ed. "It Was about Time: A Timeline of Women at UVA: A 200-Year Journey for Influence, an Education and Equality." *Virginia Magazine*, 2020, 2. Morris, Keyandra. "The Cultural Divide of Partying." *Orphée Noir*, 9 Nov. 2017.
2. Le, Judy. "Lawn Hate Crime: Noose on Homer Statue Summons FBI: Police Release Security Photos, Offer $10K for More Information." *Virginia Magazine*, 2022.
3. Baker, Lexi. "NAACP Responds to Vandalism Reported along Dawson's Row." *NAACP Responds to Vandalism Reported along Dawson's Row - The Cavalier Daily - University of Virginia's Student Newspaper*, 22 Aug. 2022.
4. Baker, Lexi, et al. "Woodson Institute and OAAA Host Teach-in to Discuss Recent Hate Crime and Vandalism." *Woodson Institute and OAAA Host Teach-in to Discuss Recent Hate Crime and Vandalism - The Cavalier Daily - University of Virginia's Student Newspaper*, 20 Sept. 2022
5. Shah, Angilee. "UVA's Very Affluent Student Body." *Charlottesville Tomorrow*, 21 July 2023.
6. Watson, Denise. "The Black Bus Stop Is a Landmark Only a Minority Knew About." *Virginia Magazine*, 2019.
7. Saul, Stephanie. "University of Virginia Suspends Tours Criticized for Emphasizing Ties to Slavery." *The New York Times*, The New York Times, 29 Aug. 2024
8. Farish, Mitch. "Behind Serpentine Walls: Centering Enslaved Laborers at Uva." *UVA Library*, 25 Jan. 2022.
9. Gordon-Reed, Annette. *Thomas Jefferson and Sally Hemings: An American Controversy.* University Press of Virginia, 1997.

Afterword
by Nsofwa Jaronda Chanda

It is an absolute privilege to offer final thoughts on *UVA Untold: Black Women's Narratives at the University of Virginia* by Cheyenne Butler. As I prepared to reflect on this powerful work, I was filled with a mix of emotions, expectations, and anticipation for what I would uncover through this qualitative research. Reading each narrative—stories of individual women that connect to the shared experiences of countless Black women navigating predominantly White spaces—reinforced truths I've known and lived for the past ten years working at UVA.

This body of work is profoundly timely, particularly as we find ourselves in a post-election America, where once again, we have witnessed the nation overlook not only the brilliance of women in general, but the exceptional contributions of a woman of color—one who identifies as both Indian and Black, and who embodies the very essence of "Black girl magic." After reading Butler's work and reflecting on the current political climate, the invisibility, lack of belonging and "othering" of which these Black women shared in *Untold*, remains painfully evident. In a society that consistently marginalizes their voices, Black women continue to be the least heard, the least protected, and one of the most vulnerable demographics in the United States of America.

As an educator, advocate, and Assistant Director at the Maxine Platzer Lynn Women's Center, I have always strived to create spaces where Black women's voices are not only heard but celebrated. Through initiatives like the *Speaking in Hues* podcast and programs such as the *Black Womanhood in College Workshop*, we've worked to provide opportunities for Black women to feel seen and supported. While these efforts have made a small difference, their reach and impact are limited; they can only touch so many lives and raise awareness to a certain extent.

Butler's work goes further—it amplifies and illuminates the complex realities that Black women face, realities that are often ignored or dismissed. This research cuts through the silence, exposing the multifaceted layers of injustice, mistreatment, and exclusion that Black women experience—not just in social spaces like parties, but also within classrooms, relationships, and professional environments. It provides a critical platform for these voices, helping to bring long-overdue visibility to the challenges and triumphs of Black women in White-dominated spaces.

I deeply admire the courage of the fifteen women featured in this study, who speak up and out against the systemic inequalities and daily microaggressions they encounter. Their stories are not just personal—they are a collective truth. But as much as I respect their willingness to share these difficult experiences, I also recognize the exhaustion that comes with being both the victimized and the educator in every instance of injustice. It is a heavy burden to carry, and often, the emotional labor of having to teach others about these realities feels endless.

What makes Butler's work so impactful is that it provides a tangible resource for Black women to point to, a space where their voices and experiences are validated, without requiring them to constantly educate or fight against the tide when they are already worn thin. In this way, *UVA Untold* serves not only as a testament to the resilience of Black women, but also as a powerful tool for change—one that allows them to be seen and heard on their own terms.

Editor Biography

Cheyenne Butler, Class of 2024

Cheyenne Butler graduated from the University of Virginia in 2024 with a B.A in History and minor in Russian Language and Literature. She is currently pursuing her J.D at Tulane University School of Law. While in university she enjoyed learning about the relationship between race, gender, and social hierarchy. Therefore, as a Black woman attending a PWI with historical ties to the plight of the Black community, Cheyenne developed this project with the explicit intent to illuminate the voices of Black undergraduate women on UVA grounds and highlight Black community and coalitions at the institution. She wanted to showcase expressions of Blackness through the experiences of Black women to further recontextualize the quintessential university experience.

She has held many undergraduate honors as a Posse Foundation Full-Tuition Scholarship Recipient, Inaugural UVA Law Roadmap Scholar Program member, USOAR scholar, Harrison Undergraduate Research Award recipient, and Corcoran Department of History Distinguished Majors Program student. During her time at UVA she found fulfillment by serving as Women's Center Intern as a writer for Iris Magazine, writer for HerCampus Magazine, writer for The Virginia Black Review, a Language Consultant for the Volunteers with International Staff, Students, and Scholars program (VISAS), and as volunteer co-organizer and mentor for The Black Womanhood in College Workshop.

In her free time, Cheyenne enjoys spending time with her family and friends, trying new restaurants, writing short stories, and making pinterest boards.

www.ingramcontent.com/pod-product-compliance
Lightning Source LLC
Chambersburg PA
CBHW021508090426
42739CB00007B/523